God and General Longstreet

God and General Longstreet

THE LOST CAUSE AND THE SOUTHERN MIND

THOMAS L. CONNELLY AND BARBARA L. BELLOWS

LOUISIANA STATE UNIVERSITY PRESS   Baton Rouge and London

Designer: Joanna Hill
Typeface: Trump
Typesetter: G & S Typesetters, Inc.
Printer and binder: Thomson-Shore, Inc.

LIBRARY OF CONGRESS CATALOGING IN PUBLICATION DATA
Connelly, Thomas Lawrence.
God and General Longstreet.
Bibliography: p.
Includes index.
1. Confederate States of America—History. 2. Southern
States in Literature. 3. Longstreet, James, 1821–1904.
4. Lee, Robert E. (Robert Edward), 1807–1870. I. Bel-
lows, Barbara L. II. Title.
E487.C798   973.7'13   782-33
ISBN 0-8071-1020-5   AACR2

To the memory of
T. Harry Williams

CONTENTS

God and General Longstreet

Chapter One

GOD AND GENERAL LONGSTREET

Those who have written about the South have played care-
lessly with the term *Lost Cause*. Well over a century has
passed since the Confederacy's demise, but the meaning of the
phrase remains as elusive as the many varying images of the
South itself. Few would question that the Civil War is, histor-
ically, the central element of the southern experience. However, by relating the approaching war to the slavery issue and
the ensuing defeat to the lasting problem of race relations in
Dixie one sees the war as *the* fomenter of attitudes south of the
Mason-Dixon line.

So it is especially ironic, even in this region where history is
beset by an overweening sense of irony, that the true meaning
of the Lost Cause has remained so nebulous. Perhaps this provides further evidence of the truth in Robert Penn Warren's observation that the southern mind does not grasp abstractions
well, but demands a sense of the concrete. Certainly there is
nothing tangible in the spirit of the Lost Cause that has slipped
blithely through the time and space of generations of southerners. Over the years the meaning has varied. Some writers have
used it to describe the literary outpouring from that angry ca-
dre of former-Rebel political and military luminaries, represented by such men as Jefferson Davis, Alexander H. Stephens,
P. G. T. Beauregard. In the years after Appomattox, they labored to justify secession, defend unfortunate decisions, and

rationalize defeat. These writers represented the "diehard" mentality evident in Dixie between 1865 and the Great War. This was the generation that raised shafts of Italian marble on the lawns of southern courthouses, marched feebly in ever-decreasing numbers to the evocative drumbeats at Confederate reunions, and fought out the war in pitiable veterans' magazines. Despite hard times they always found money for their United Confederate Veterans dues or the opportunity to spend Wednesday afternoon with their gray-haired friends, United Daughters.

There is another, broader definition that has portrayed the Lost Cause as a timeless ideal, free of the limitations of space and time. Here the imagery has been used to encompass many things: the bitter, turgid political rationales penned by a sickly Jefferson Davis; hoarse Rebel yells in reunion halls filled with aged veterans; Thomas Nelson Page's Virginia "massa" with his ancient, wise, and ever-loyal servant; the Confederate flags still flying over southern capitals; or even the Rebel Band of Ole Miss as it proudly marches to the strains of "Dixie."

The origins of the phrase are easier to understand. Southern romanticism of the early nineteenth century had thrived upon Sir Walter Scott's accounts of the lost cause of Scotland in its quest for independence. An antebellum South embroiled in a power struggle with the "churlish Saxons" of Yankeedom could identify with a heroic Ivanhoe. Small wonder it was that the Rebel battleflag adopted the design of the Scottish St. Andrew's cross, or that Dixie writers during the Reconstruction era attempted to link the ancestry of Robert E. Lee with that of Robert the Bruce. The shrewd Ohio observer Albion Tourgée speculated that "the down-fall of empire is always the epoch of romance."

So the phrase developed soon after Appomattox as a byword for the perpetuation of the Confederate ideal. The first important Confederate historian, wartime journalist Edward Pollard, adopted it as the title of his first major postwar study of the Rebel experience. Pollard's *The Lost Cause* (1866) foretold a coming generation of writers committed to justifying the southern experience. His concise title belies the difficulties of understanding exactly what Lost Cause is supposed to mean. One could suggest that it embodied the mental processes of an entire generation of southerners in the late nineteenth century. Many such southerners were involved in Confederate military and political circles. So they attempted, during the years of defeat, to justify secession and military catastrophe. Some were politicians and generals, such as Jefferson Davis or Jubal Early; others were poets, novelists, and professional journalists such as Edward Pollard, John Esten Cooke, and many others. Their literary talents, good and bad, spoke for a larger body of their fellow southerners who lacked the public means to express the frustrations caused by a mosaic of defeat, poverty, and social upheaval.

On the surface, these frustrations gradually ebbed. The passing of time quieted the roar of Rebel yells in veterans' reunion camps, reduced the ranks of the United Confederate Veterans, and stilled the often vituperous pens of the most unyielding Confederate authors. There also came a softening of attitudes between the blue and the gray. By the turn of the century, the old combatants were just that—white-haired, tottering old men, often feeble and armed with canes instead of rifled muskets. They gathered in poignant encampments such as the 1913 Gettysburg reunion, and in the shadow of the Great War, clung to one another, strangely out of place in a world of mustard gas, airplanes, and machine guns. In touching episodes they were passing from the scene—the deaf, nearly blind General James Longstreet, unable to hear the thunderous applause as the audience gathered for the 1902 centennial observance at West Point; baldheaded General Joe Johnston, who became ill and later died after standing hatless at the funeral of his old adversary General William Sherman; the cheers of a quarter of a million people gathered along Pennsylvania Avenue in 1917 when Confederate veterans paraded with signs reading, "Send us if the boys can't do the job." Somewhere in these years, the formal posture of an alienated Confederate people dissolved into a mellow sense of reunion. It marked the end of a generation that had espoused the Lost Cause.

There is another body of opinion that would suggest that the Lost Cause did not end with the former Confederates or their children. Was the Lost Cause something greater in time and space, perhaps the core of that enduring memory of southern defeat? The larger definition encompasses more than the idealized romanticism of the authors of the postwar years.

It becomes, instead, an enduring blend of romance and tragedy that the southern literary critic Walter Sullivan viewed as one of the strengths of the southern renascence in the 1930s. One is inclined to agree with Sullivan's argument that the novels of William Faulkner, Robert Penn Warren, and others reflect an ambivalence of view in the modern southerner's mind about his past. It becomes what Wallace Stevens described in another context as the "rage for order," a search for a system of beliefs in the aristocratic legend of the Old South. When observed in this context, the Lost Cause becomes that enduring memory of Confederate loss inscribed on Faulkner's courthouse-square clock in *Intruder in the Dust*. It also becomes C. Vann Woodward's study of the southern mind's burden of defeat; Caroline Gordon's search for order among the old values in *None Shall Look Back*; and Carson McCullers' metaphor of the conflict between individualism and order in *Member of the Wedding*.

These two definitions of the Lost Cause, so varied in time and purpose, are not at all irreconcilable. The solution to the enigma of the phrase might come in accepting the existence of two such phenomena. Both lost causes were interpreted by separate bodies of writers who at once reflected the contemporary

southern outlook on the Civil War and helped to fashion opinion. The National Lost Cause, which will be described in a
later essay, originated in the late nineteenth century as a literary endeavor to interpret the place of the South within the nation. From its first efforts in the writings of local colorists such
as George Cary Eggleston, Sara Pryor, and Thomas Nelson
Page, it was bidimensional in the attempt to explain the meaning of the Confederate experience to outsiders as well as to
southerners.

The Inner Lost Cause describes a mentality that arose from
the ashes of defeat, fought for three decades in print and oratory, and dwindled in the shadow of the First World War. These
were the people who manned the veterans' organizations, former Rebel generals, such as Beauregard and Joseph Johnston,
who more often than not fought among themselves as they
gave reasons for Yankee defeat.

One cannot appreciate fully the influence of these writers on
southern letters without understanding two important matters. First, the Inner Lost Cause boasted a high degree of organization that gave both strength and endurance. This literary
surge, which spoke for the southern mood, was far more than
the lonely efforts of bitter former politicians and generals who
whiled away the years after Appomattox penning angry diatribes. Instead, the Inner Lost Cause marshaled the resources of
numerous magazines, organizations, and even pulpits.

The avenues of public outcry were far flung. The Confederate rationale was preached through the powerful *Southern Historical Society Papers* and other magazines such as the *Southern Review, The Land We Love,* the *Confederate Veteran,* and
Southern Bivouac. In turn, the Rebel veterans were also well
organized. At first, during the Reconstruction era, the structure
involved local units and armywide groups such as the influential Association of the Army of Northern Virginia. Then the
United Confederate Veterans emerged in 1889; within fifteen

years the association could claim 80,000 members—at least one-third of all surviving Rebel soldiers.

These magazines and veterans' groups represented only the top layer of a complex web of organizations that kept alive the Confederate mentality for decades after Appomattox. There were some associations organized throughout the entire South, such as the influential Southern Historical Society, the Lee Memorial Association, and the Lee Monument Association. Scores of other local and subregional groups were also committed to the task of commemorating Confederate heroes. Numerous women's organizations, all dedicated to the preservation of the Confederate memory, eventually united into the Confederate Memorial Association, while the rival United Daughters of the Confederacy enjoyed a thriving membership. The rising tide of evangelical faith, witnessed in the phenomenal growth of the Southern Baptist Church and other fundamentalist churches, gave solace and structure to the defeated Confederate generation. Meanwhile, textbooks for young schoolchildren were supervised by watchdog committees of veterans' organizations, so that young southern minds would be taught the "true history" of the War Between the States.

Yet organization alone does not explain the power of this effort. The emotional drive that underscored several decades of writing and oratory was incredibly strong. Here is the great difference between the ambitions of the Confederate mentality reflected in the Inner Lost Cause and the more pragmatic reunion-oriented southern authors of the later National Lost Cause. The generation of Jefferson Davis and Jubal Early possessed a quality of anger that wrought a one-dimensional approach. Until after 1900, when the parting literary shots were fired by the last of this group, the Confederates of the Inner Lost Cause wrote more to appease their own frustrations and fears than to convert a national audience.

In fact, it sometimes appeared that the former Rebels cared

little what a northern audience thought of their efforts. The old boasts, prejudices, and grandiose arguments that compared Confederate greatness with Yankee amorality, boorishness, and even cowardice still appeared in veterans' magazines in the early twentieth century.

Certainly these former Confederates cared deeply how the rest of the world viewed the southern cause of 1861. The desire to be vindicated in the nation's eyes was a prime motive for the organization of the Southern Historical Society in 1869. The society—and other organizations—sought to collect war records and publish southern accounts of the war so that the truth would be known. As a speaker observed at a Savannah reunion meeting in 1883, "the gathering and the publishing of the records of the war are the essential justification of our cause."

The essential factor is that the Inner Lost Cause artists did not expect exculpation in *their* time. The speeches and articles of the Confederate generation are dominated by a certain air of resignation, almost religious in nature, that redemption would come in time. General Daniel Harvey Hill, editor of *The Land We Love*, mused that "mists and fogs may obscure the sun for a season, but there will come a time of meridian brightness and glory" when the Confederate cause would be justified. "Stonewall" Jackson's former chief of staff, Robert L. Dabney, expressed the same sentiment in an 1868 speech, when he observed that "the vision of the harvest . . . may tarry; but in the end it will not fail and we will wait for it."

Even more to the point was General Wade Hampton's address to the Washington Artillery of Charleston in 1878, with the same mixture of religion and redemption. Hampton, looking forward to the vindication of the Confederacy, assured his comrades that "right *shall* make might my friends. We may not see it here on earth, where truth so often goes down before falsehood . . . but in the last great reckoning . . . you who have stood by this right shall on that day find that right shall prevail." All three former Confederate officers reflected that great expectation of the Inner Lost Cause that redemption would come eventually. Victory would at last be theirs.

What did they wish to redeem? Probably the architects of the Lost Cause wished to retrieve *something* from a sense of both calamity and estrangement. The calamities of physical loss and social change experienced by the postwar South are well documented. Over a quarter of a million men perished in the war, several million suffered wounds, and many were maimed physically or emotionally for life. In Mississippi, for example, one-third of the white men of military age were killed or crippled; one-fifth of that state's revenue in 1866 was expended on artificial limbs for war amputees.

Physical destruction was present everywhere. Most important, southern towns lay in ruins or had suffered extensive physical damage. Prime agricultural areas such as the fertile Shenandoah Valley of Virginia were left in desolation. Two-thirds of the South's rail network had been destroyed, homes proud and humble were in a shambles, and once-choice plantation soil fell before the auctioneer's gavel at two dollars an acre.

Social disruption was no less calamitous. Several million former slaves moved among their former masters at will, voting and holding office. Literary and cultural centers at Charleston and New Orleans would never regain past glory. Southern educational systems were in disarray. Worse, much of the South's leadership class had disappeared.

The South of 1861 was caste conscious, and placed its faith with the political orator or the military chieftain. The armies organized to fight at Bull Run and elsewhere were dominated by the old political-military leadership class, down to the colonels and lieutenant colonels who led regiments, and even to company officers. Of the 425 Confederate general officers, only 125 were professional soldiers, whereas 260 came to service after careers in politics and law or as jurists, planters, or businessmen.

Almost a fourth of the South's general officers perished in the war, and many of these had been community leaders. There was Roger Hanson, the prominent Kentucky legislator and attorney, who was shot down in the battle of Stone's River; General Patrick Cleburne, who died leading his division at Franklin, Tennessee, was a well-known attorney and businessman in Helena, Arkansas. Thomas Cobb, who bled to death after being wounded in the sunken road at Fredericksburg, was a constitutional lawyer of great reputation in Georgia and had compiled a new state criminal code shortly before the war erupted.

Battlefield issues did not wholly explain the leadership vacuum. A number of once-prominent generals and politicians fled the defeated Confederacy and sought exile in England, France, Mexico, Venezuela, Cuba, New Zealand, Brazil, and elsewhere. Secretary of State Judah P. Benjamin moved his residence to Paris. The eminent Kentucky politician and Rebel war secretary, John C. Breckinridge, went to England. Six thousand former Rebels migrated to Brazil, over two thousand went into Mexico, and hundreds more escaped to Venezuela and British Honduras.

The loss of talent and the old leadership class can be observed in the single colony of Confederates at Carlotta, Mexico. At Carlotta were such notables as General Thomas Hindman, former Arkansas congressman and division leader at Chickamauga; the former congressman and Missouri governor General Sterling Price; the wartime governor of Tennessee, Isham Harris; the former Louisiana governor Henry Watkins Allen; Generals Jo Shelby and John Bankhead Magruder, prominent in the war theater west of the Mississippi; and General Walter Stevens, former chief engineer of Robert E. Lee's Army of Northern Virginia. Stevens' engineering skill was sorely needed in repairing Virginia's shattered rail system; instead, he worked as superintendent and chief engineer of the Mexican Imperial Railway.

One of those who sulked in a Montreal hotel lobby was General Jubal Early. Early was a stereotype of the basic paradoxical nature of the southern mind. A prominent Virginia attorney, he had fought against secession in 1861. But when Virginia left the Union, he became the most rebellious of all Rebels—a crude, profane "Yankee-hating" individual.

However, after Appomattox, Jubal Early deserted his comrades. For a time he wandered like an Ishmael, through Mexico, Cuba, and Canada. Meanwhile, he wrote pitiful letters to his old commander, Robert E. Lee, who had become president of the struggling Washington College. The letters are filled with braggadocio and diatribes against northerners but between the lines display the guilt of one who obviously felt that he had deserted the South in a period of crisis.

Certainly Robert E. Lee saw through the veil of bravado in Early's correspondence. His poignant replies were tactful and considerate, assuring his old "Bad Man"—as Lee fondly called him—that each man must do what he believed was right. Still, in the many quiet hours when he rode his mare, Lucy Long, or the gray war-horse, Traveller, out into the Shenandoah countryside, Lee surely must have wondered—as did other former Rebels—what had happened to the Earlys, the Benjamins, the Breckinridges, and others of their class who had not remained in Dixie—and what might have happened had they not left.

The greatest calamity was the absolute shock of defeat. A nation that worshiped success was spiritually unprepared for the trauma of being the loser.

Long before the war began, the groundwork for the unrealistic optimism of 1861 was prepared. The cultural isolation of the Old South allowed the populace to exist within a fantasy world of utter contempt for the Yankee and absolute confidence in southern might.

There was ultimate faith in the military and political leadership of the planter class with its display of southern arrogance. Even the yeoman farmer or plantation overseer could aspire to membership in such a caste system, with its trappings of chivalry, an excess of military schools, and its absolute confidence in southern manhood.

The martial ardor of the early months of 1861 only intensified confidence. Most southerners doubtless shared the sentiment of the war clerk John B. Jones, who muttered, "How much better it would have been if the North had permitted the South to depart in peace!" They had all come forward, now, to the Tennessee and Virginia war zones, in companies and regiments with names such as the Tallapoosa Thrashers and Southern Avengers.

Yet beneath the indoctrination in chivalry and the fervor of 1861 was something far deeper. Even the letters of the mild-mannered Robert E. Lee describe "the evil designs of the North," an enemy that sought to reduce the Confederacy to "abject slavery." One thing is certain; as the Civil War progressed, the southern quest became involved in far more than military defeat of the North. Northern aims broadened from a restoration of the Union to aspirations of social and political reorganization of the South. As the war intensified and the issues increased in complexity, southerners became more recalcitrant. The Civil War became a jihad, a holy war, against the decay of northern industrialization, the mongrel races from Europe that swelled Yankee ranks, Jacobin theories of excessive democracy and racial disorder.

It is clear also that the southern confidence in victory was no mere braggart impulse of an agrarian society isolated from the realities of the growing industrial might of the American nation. It came instead from the wellspring of southern piety. The antebellum South remained the most puritan of all American regions, and was an exaggeration of that general American faith that there is a correlation between Jehovah's grace and success. The belief that God was on the side of the Confederacy was universal south of the Potomac.

Even in the hard days of 1862, when General George Mc-Clellan's huge army hammered at Richmond's gates, the editor of one Atlanta newspaper asserted that "our cause is just, and a righteous Judge and the God of Battles will decide in our favor." The Seven Days' was won, and soon after, Lee wrought victory again on the battlefield of Second Manassas. So a correspondent for a Savannah newspaper could eulogize that "never since Adam was planted in the garden of Eden, did a holier cause engage the hearts of any nation. Is not the hand of God in all this?" Meanwhile, Jefferson Davis said that at Manassas, "our armies have been blessed by the Lord of hosts," who provided "this great deliverance."

The war was going harder by 1863, but the Cromwellian zeal gave no sign of weakness. In the spring of 1863, when the Confederacy was threatened everywhere, from Vicksburg to Virginia, one Atlanta journalist explained, "We have to endure these atrocities of our fiendish foe, but we still believe . . . that HE chasteneth those whom he loveth, and that, in HIS own good time, HE will deliver the South from its oppressors." Even the death of the revered "Stonewall" Jackson did not dim the faith. A week after Jackson's death, another Georgia editor reminded his readers that many good generals remained, and that "above all, we have the blessing of Almighty God on as righteous a cause as the sun ever shone upon."

The same conviction is observed even in 1864, when the massive Federal double offensive moved against the Confederates in Virginia and Georgia. In April, when President Davis had called for a day of prayer, another Georgia editor reminded his readers, "We should not forget, in this critical moment, the great *Source* and *Dispenser* of Victories." When the news of Grant's casualties in the Wilderness campaign reached the Richmond press, the editor of the *Sentinel* urged his readers to thank God, because a few more days of battle "will bring us full deliverance."

But when deliverance did not come, many Rebels agreed with the sentiment of a Confederate nurse, Kate Cumming, who wrote in her diary, "Our sins must have been great to have deserved such punishment." To southerners, the belief in the superiority of their military prowess and faith in Divine Providence were inseparable. There seems little doubt that even in the last hard campaign of 1864–1865, many Confederates still believed that God would give them victory. Even in the midsummer of 1864, when Grant pushed closer to Richmond, a local editor would boast, "How can the Washington Government hope for the conquest of the Confederate States when their armies are thus annually defeated and driven back?"

Yet by the winter of 1863, there was an obvious change in the southern mood. Pulpit oratory and newspaper editorials had begun to link Yankee military success with a spiritual failure on the part of southerners. Within months, the fortunes of war had turned sharply against the Confederacy. Vicksburg was gone, Chattanooga had surrendered, and Robert E. Lee's once-vaunted army had been shattered at Gettysburg. After the war, George Cary Eggleston recalled that in those grim days, "the men had ceased to rely upon the skill of our leaders or the strength of our army for success," and turned instead to religion.

The Great Revival that swept the Confederate camps in the winter of 1863–1864 never has been appreciated fully by observers of the southern mind. It was a massive outburst of evangelical religion, not unlike the Great Revival of 1801 on the frontier. In army camps from Virginia to Texas, Rebel soldiers by the tens of thousands became religious converts. In Virginia, whole brigades stood barefoot in several inches of snow to hear chaplains warn that the military reverses proved that Jehovah was angry with the Confederacy. Log tabernacles were erected in the lines of General Joe Johnston's army in Georgia. Before Sherman's bluecoats advanced on Johnston in the Atlanta campaign, the religious fervor had touched even the high command of the Army of Tennessee. During the spring of 1864, Episcopal Bishop Leonidas Polk, one of the army's corps leaders, baptized almost everyone in the upper echelons, including Johnston and Generals John Bell Hood and William Hardee.

Consider again the remark by nurse Cumming that Confederate sins "must have been great to have deserved such punishment." Her conviction was no different from that expressed by Robert E. Lee in the winter of 1863, when he could see the tide turning on the eastern front. Lee mused, "We do not know what is best for us. I believe a kind God has ordered all things for our good." The same theology was expressed in 1863 by an Atlanta editor who mourned that while for a time the South must endure Yankee victories, "we still believe, nay, have an *abiding faith* that HE chasteneth those whom he loveth, and that, in HIS own good time, HE will deliver the South from its oppressors."

When God did not grant the deliverance, southerners felt that they were experiencing a vast calamity. Reading through the political and patriotic rhetoric of postwar military apologies or historical justifications for secession, one views something far deeper than the literary polemics of men who were confused, angry, and frustrated by defeat. In essence, the South was spiritually unprepared for Appomattox.

Sometimes these men admitted this later. In 1878 a veteran recalled "I had no glimmering foresight of the cataclysm. I felt quite confident that the Day of Judgement would come before

Richmond would pass into the possession of the enemy." Another survivor of Appomattox, Edward Boykin, reminisced that "those of us who took serious consideration of the state of affairs felt that without defeat we had absolutely lost our country."

Better yet, go back to George Cary Eggleston's serialized memoir, "A Rebel's Recollections," in the *Atlantic Monthly.* Eggleston recalled that even in the 1864 campaign, when Ulysses S. Grant's columns of Federal infantry appeared endless, Lee's veterans refused to admit possible failure. Instead, "We were convinced, beyond the possibility of a doubt, of the absolute righteousness of our cause, and in spite of history we persuaded ourselves that a people battling for the right could not fail in the end." There was more. Eggleston also remarked that it was "our religion to believe in the triumph of our cause, and it was heresy of the rankest sort to doubt it or even to admit the possibility of failure."

One wonders whether modern observers of the Reconstruction South have fully comprehended the implications of Eggleston's observations. He reflected the spiritual and emotional sense of calamity shared by an entire defeated generation. Still, few writers have probed the depths of this psychological trauma that did much to inspire the Lost Cause mentality.

Certainly the agonies often listed by historians were real ones—the abject poverty, the disruption of the old social and racial order, and the vast changes in Dixie's political fabric. It may be, however, that Eggleston and his generation viewed such problems not as the end result, but only as evidences of a greater catastrophe. After all, the postwar South was no stranger to hard economic times. Life was hard for many southerners before the war, and four years of war already had produced economic despair.

Nor were southerners in 1865 totally unprepared for social and political change. Alterations in the South's cultural and political fabric had begun long before Appomattox. Nashville, Memphis, and New Orleans fell to the enemy in early 1862. Vast stretches of the northern border in Kentucky, Tennessee, Missouri, and western Virginia were under Yankee dominance by 1863, as were parts of Mississippi, Alabama, Louisiana, Florida, and the Carolinas. For several million southerners, existence in a Confederacy apart from the old Union was a short-lived affair. When Lee surrendered, for example, Nashville had been under Union control for over three years.

Still, the Reconstruction generation may have viewed such misfortune as evidences of a far greater calamity, that of *estrangement* from their Creator. If so, the entire genre of Lost Cause literature possessed theological and psychological undertones. Beneath the realities of poverty, social disruption, and political readjustment, there was something far more difficult to reconcile. This was the awful prospect that God had turned His back upon the Confederacy.

The very nature of southern piety in the years after Appomattox could have produced this sense of alienation. A general pattern of southern Protestant thought already had emerged in the antebellum period. It came out of the religious ferment of the Great Awakening in the previous century, and from the Great Revival that swept the American frontier after 1801. Already by 1800 the victors were the left-wing dissenting groups such as the Baptist, Methodist, and New Light Presbyterian faiths that claimed the souls of most southerners.

After the Great Revival of 1801, southern religious patterns became even more deeply embedded in the new revival faiths. Certainly the entire American West at first shared in the emotional fervor and heavy emphasis upon personal salvation. After all, the hardships and insecurities of the frontier experience were not regional problems. Emotional fervor and individualism combined to produce a strong evangelical force that emphasized voluntarism. The core of the new frontier faith was the emphasis upon personal salvation. God was no longer an abstract deity to be worshiped. He was now a constant presence, who offered salvation to those who accepted the faith.

By the 1840s southern religion was dominated heavily by such thinking. Frontier evangelism dwindled in the North during this period, and the frontier itself gave way to a more urban and cosmopolitan society. The diversities of the reform impulse, a new wave of immigration, and other factors also contributed to the decline of evangelical revivalism north of the Potomac River.

Meanwhile, the new evangelical faith was becoming more firmly entrenched in the South. The psychological impact of the frontier remained a real force, as did the accompanying features of poverty, lack of education, and peculiar southern individualism. Some older Dixie faiths such as the Episcopal church continued to lose strength. Even the Presbyterian church, also possessed of more formal structure, could not keep pace with the fervor of the Baptist and Methodist churches that in the early eighteenth-century South, were almost nonexistent. By the time of the Civil War, they were the South's largest denominations.

In both theology and church structure, the postwar South embraced a religious credo that would affect greatly the Lost Cause rationale. Like most aspects of the southern mind, it was a paradox. In this case, the dichotomy was a mixture of individualism and collectivism. Salvation and voluntarism became inseparable. Like traditional Calvinistic faith in America, the southern evangelicals believed that man was, in one sense, opposed to God, his initial status that of a doomed sinner, banned from God's presence. The sacrifice of Christ had provided the means of pardon.

But unlike the standard Calvinist faith, the southern version, born out of frontier individualism, made man the prime agent of his own salvation. In effect, the religion of the Lost Cause generation was man-centered. The southern concept of the Trinity was not the Father, Son, and Holy Spirit, but God, man, and Satan. Man was a battleground between good and evil, and he alone controlled his final destiny. Once man accepted Christ and was saved, he was no longer estranged from the Almighty.

The theology exalted the individual's relationship to God, but the road to salvation was a collective one. The church became the place where one lived out his quest for salvation. As Samuel Hill, Jr., points out in *Southern Churches in Crisis*, almost every other traditional function of the established church was subordinated totally to the evangelical zeal to save the lost. Worship services did not concentrate upon veneration for a deity, but reaffirmed one's companionship with God as a personal savior. The music of these evangelical churches did not center upon hymns of praise to God, but upon revival and "gospel" songs that reminded the erring sinner that salvation's choice was his own.

Likewise, social and community responsibility was never a part of the evangelical southern faith, before or after the Civil War. Obviously, such churches supported the status quo of prevailing southern institutions. Not only was slavery defended from the pulpits, but the churches themselves joined the sectional controversy.

It was more a withdrawing into the confines of their own religious credo and sectional faith. By the 1850s the three basic evangelical faiths had seceded and formed their own regional organizations: Southern Baptist; the Methodist Episcopal Church, South; and the (Southern) Presbyterian Church in the United States.

Immediately after the Civil War, the retreat from the mainstream continued. By the 1880s white southern Baptists and southern Methodists had segregated white and black church members into separate organization and congregations, and the southern Presbyterians by 1900 had also instituted segregation.

Just as Dixie's religion could defend—or ignore—the presence of slavery, so, too, could it overlook the South's deeper social problems after the Civil War. One might speculate that the total obsession of popular southern religion with personal salvation—before and after Appomattox—was a matter of putting all one's guilt into the proverbial basket. It may have been easier to cope with the overview of man as a sinner than to delineate acts of wrongdoing, such as slavery, secession, segregation, and others.

There appears to be a strong connection between the Lost Cause mentality and the increasing strength of evangelical religion in the postwar South. One recalls an often-quoted remark by a Mississippi preacher after Appomattox, that "if we cannot gain our *political* [independence], let us establish at least our *mental* independence."

Certainly such separatism developed in the four decades after 1865. There was a huge increase in the rolls of evangelical churches. By 1906 over one-half (3.26 million) of the South's 6.2 million white churchmen were either Southern Baptists or members of the Methodist Episcopal Church, South. Almost another million parishioners were members of other conservative faiths—Southern Presbyterian, Church of Christ, Disciples of Christ and the rising tide of Pentecostal and Holiness sects.

A generation of former Confederates could find solace in such religion. Supported by devotion to biblical literalism and church orthodoxy, such groups were absolutely one-dimensional in their approach. The key concern was "what must I do to be saved?"

Yet one might argue that this surge of evangelical zeal did not equip southerners to handle the problem of defeat in the Civil War. Of course, there were other matters, outside the sphere of religion, that made it difficult to cope with Appomattox. There was the awareness of being denied the American dream of success, of finding oneself alienated from the Calvinistic belief that God blesses the righteous.

Another impediment to the panacea of postwar religion was the nature of the neoclassical southern mind. The belief in a personal, fixed relationship between man and his Creator was universal in the South, and transcended membership in some sectarian body. This was an element of regional piety that rested on matters much deeper than church labels. Since God and man were united in a close personal bond, the intervention of the Creator in human affairs was a daily event. An Episcopalian such as General Robert E. Lee also believed firmly in this God-man relationship, in man's striving for salvation beyond a transient earthly existence, and in the daily intercession of Jehovah in man's affairs.

And when victory did not come, the evangelical faith left the former Confederates unprepared to accept loss. The core of postwar southern religion was more than a quest for salvation. It involved the need to believe that an individual *was* saved. One's status with God was a personal, emotional matter. Long ago the Puritans had abandoned John Calvin's belief that one's relationship to God was in part decided by his participation in sacraments, and had concluded that avowals of faith and moral uprightness were the tests of whether one was of the elect.

By the nineteenth century, paradoxically, southern religion had liberalized the old puritan tests of faith. Formal rituals of conversion and public displays of "good works" were subordinated to a transcendental belief that the evidence of grace existed within the individual mind. The criterion for salvation had become the highly subjective element of feeling and emotion. Now the assurance of one's "being right with God" was a highly personal matter, dependent upon the individual's own feeling.

Given this theological and philosophical background, it is not surprising that the postwar southern generation was unprepared for the reality of defeat. Their pervasive sense of alienation involved a sense of estrangement from God, the American doctrine of success, the mainstream of national life, and even from themselves.

The Inner Lost Cause movement was a reaction to this sense of intellectual displacement. It lasted for over fifty years although the prime emotional drive was demonstrated in the two decades after Appomattox. The battle was fought in the *Southern Historical Society Papers, Our Living and Our Dead, Southern Bivouac, The Land We Love, Southern Magazine, Southern Review,* and later the *Confederate Veteran.* It was a topic of speeches given at veterans' groups such as the Association of the Army of Northern Virginia, and at the dedication ceremonies for monuments to such Confederate heroes as Albert Sidney Johnston, "Stonewall" Jackson, and Robert E. Lee. The arguments filled the pages of political memoirs by Jefferson Davis, Alexander Stephens, and others. Even the plethora of reminiscences written by the Confederate generals must be considered as part of the Lost Cause literature.

This huge collection of books, articles, and orations possessed one central theme, and it was best expressed by Edward Pollard in *The Lost Cause.* During the war, Pollard's acid pen often expressed scorn for the Confederate government. On occasion he even had ventured to criticize General Robert E. Lee. Still, the Richmond newspaperman was totally orthodox in his appraisal of the touchstone of the Lost Cause. To Pollard, the South remained superior "in all the standards of individual character over the people of the North"; southerners were "the better men."

This quality of moral self-assertion, or better said, moral reinforcement, was the basic theme of the literature and oratory of the Inner Lost Cause. Both traditional southern piety and the new evangelism stressed the close relationship between God and man. The new tide of conservative faiths placed squarely upon the individual the burden of proof that he was one of the elect. There were no outward tests—only the highly personal matter of whether the believer "felt right."

How could one feel redeemed when God had failed to provide succor for Robert E. Lee's army? Any direction to which southerners could turn brought only entrapment in guilt and doubt. The puritan ethic had taught them the relationship between success and God's grace while basic southern piety stressed God's personal closeness and intervention in man's affairs. The new evangelism in effect preached that one's feeling of inner peace was the only evidence of salvation, while the increasing popularity of Darwinism and pragmatism extolled the survival-of-the-fittest institutions and the relationship between achievement and merit.

Confused, and not a little angry, the postwar generation of southerners fought back with almost grotesque assertions of their moral superiority. This was the absolute heart of the Inner Lost Cause rationale, that whatever had occurred, southerners were still the *better men.*

Every one of the arguments was buttressed by the moral factor. The political apology for secession was expressed in turgid prose. Jefferson Davis spent over two hundred pages in the first volume of his *The Rise and Fall of the Confederate Government* in an attempt to prove that the South was the rightful heir to the traditions of the Revolutionary forefathers. Alexander Stephens used this argument as the basis for his *A Constitutional View of the Late War Between the States* (1868) as did Alfred Bledsoe's 1866 apology, *Is Davis a Traitor, or Was Secession a Constitutional Right Previous to 1861?*

On the surface, the political apologists were concerned with the historical and constitutional right of secession. Their underlying theme, however, was the issue of political morality.

The South had adhered to the virtues of the Revolutionary generation and the authors of the Constitution. It was the North that had violated the Constitution by attacks upon the expansion of slavery, states' rights, and other issues. Now the postwar North was devoted to a political Jacobinism and belief in rule by the masses over state interests, which violated the traditions of the founders. Even during the war, the rationale was already present in an editorial in the Atlanta *Daily Intelligencer*, which asserted that since 1776, "men have risen up in the North who knew not our forefathers, but have departed from their ways and have basely violated the compact made with their Southern brethren."

The *better-men* concept also proposed that the war had been a grand epic fought by a chivalrous South. The trappings of the self-image of a knightly Confederacy were visible for decades after the surrender. By the 1870s, the tournament had been revived as a popular sport. The ornamental trappings were often shabby and the horses less than thoroughbreds, but the belief in a southern chivalry had not diminished. A writer in the *Southern Historical Society Papers* praised "the chivalric deeds" of General "Jeb" Stuart, the "Chevalier Bayard" of the Confederacy.

In part the chivalric resurgence was a blend of escapism and nostalgia. After all, the war had called young men from drab existences in backwater communities and lonely rural areas to march in huge armies. For most of them, it was the one great experience of their lives. In defeat, they had returned home to a culture made even more drab by the hardships of war. The more removed these men were from the war's horrors, the more fanciful became their image of the conflict. If nothing else, the chivalric image provided escape from harsh realities.

Typical was the attitude of a Georgia cavalry officer, Colonel I. W. Avery, who published his war reminiscences in 1868. At first his account displayed only the flamboyant imagery of chivalry. He spoke of wartime ventures "on our plunging steed," while "iron blade clashes against blade." Then Colonel Avery drew back, almost half-embarrassed, and admitted that a former Rebel must view the war in this fashion, since "he has but his misfortunes and honor left to him." So "he drowns the gloomy recollection of disaster" in an opiate of the romantic epic, so that "the desolate present is forgotten."

Still, beneath this escapism was the moral element. The central figure was the Christian knight, who had made war against a host of outside foes—political Jacobinism, irreligion, and human greed. Years after the surrender, another former Rebel cavalryman, General W. H. Jackson spoke at a tournament held in Nashville, Tennessee, to raise funds for a Confederate memorial. His speech underscored the close ties between Christianity and the chivalric code. Jackson compared Christendom's invasion of Islam with the Confederacy's struggle against northern vandals. Thus, "where the moral suasion of the Church failed, the sword of the knight was mighty to convince and reform the tyrant and robber."

The *better-men* concept dominated also the deluge of military reminiscences written by former Confederates, but obviously there were other motives for the onrush of war memoirs. General John Bell Hood's *Advance and Retreat* was both a defense of his own generalship and an attack upon his predecessor in the western command, Joseph Johnston. In turn, Johnston's own *Narrative of Military Operations* castigated both Hood and another hated foe, Jefferson Davis. Davis in *The Rise and Fall of the Confederate Government* assailed Johnston and another favorite culprit, General P. G. T. Beauregard. Meanwhile, Beauregard fought back against Davis by supplying rough drafts for use by his handpicked biographer, Alfred Roman, for the *Military Operations of General Beauregard*.

Scores of such military debates held a meaning beyond the issue of personal pride. These men differed on the finer points of battle tactics, but shared the common belief that Confederate leadership was far superior to northern command. The men believed this foremost because they were southern humanists who feared that an analysis of defeat would weaken the entire fabric. It was essential in their credo to accept Pollard's *bettermen* concept. To think otherwise would suggest a surrender to the Yankee argument that winning was the test of truth.

So they conjured up the argument that the Confederacy was not defeated, but was overrun by northern hordes. Until well after 1900 it remained a familiar refrain of the Inner Lost Cause. The South had better generals, who were worn down eventually by endless waves of soldiers in blue, many of them accused of being European mercenaries. Even Gettysburg would be transformed from a Rebel disaster into a drawn battle.

Understandably, the wellspring of the overwhelmed-but-never-defeated imagery was Robert E. Lee. By 1865, without question, Lee was the South's most dominant military figure. After he assumed command of the Army of Northern Virginia in 1862, Lee had either damaged or demolished completely the military reputations of several opponents. General George McClellan's massive army had been driven from the Peninsula in the summer of 1862, followed by John Pope's humiliation at the battle of Second Manassas. Ambrose Burnside came to grief at Fredericksburg, and his successor, Joseph Hooker, watched while the army that he boasted was the finest on the planet was whipped soundly by Lee's vastly outnumbered Rebels at Chancellorsville.

Still, Robert E. Lee's reputation as the invincible Confederate general was a postwar phenomenon. For well over a year after the bombardment at Fort Sumter, he was certainly no household word in the Confederacy. Lee's first wartime military venture in the western Virginia campaign fared badly, and even Richmond newspapers heaped scorn upon "Granny Lee," the man of "showy presence" but little action. Some editorialists guffawed again when Lee in late 1861 was assigned command of the lower Atlantic slope, and there is evidence that prominent civil and military leaders in the region expressed doubt publicly about his abilities. Even after Lee assumed command of the Army of Northern Virginia in the early summer of 1862, one Richmond journalist hooted that "Evacuating Lee, who has never yet risked a battle with the invader," was now responsible for the city's fate.

The victory over McClellan's army in the Seven Days' campaign and later successes in 1862–1863 still did not produce an image of Lee as the total Confederate hero symbol. Throughout the war, Confederate newspapers still treated other officers— living or dead—as Lee's equals. Generals Albert Sidney Johnston, P. G. T. Beauregard, Joseph Johnston, and "Stonewall" Jackson were clearly rivals for popularity in the South. This was true especially in the case of Jackson, whose Shenandoah Valley exploits in the spring of 1862 had made him a hero in the Confederacy when Lee was virtually unknown. Even a year later, when Jackson was killed leading a corps in Lee's army, one Atlanta newspaper described him as "the idol of the people and the army," and a Richmond editor questioned, "Who can fill his place in our hearts?"

Robert E. Lee's postwar emergence as the *invincible* military leader resulted partly out of an enthusiastic cult of followers in Virginia that coalesced after the General's death in 1870. Already Virginia had become the focus of southern letters, replacing the moribund literary centers of Charleston and New Orleans. The Southern Historical Society, along with its influential journal, fell under the control of Lee devotees such as his former corps leader Jubal Early, his nephew Fitzhugh Lee, former staff officers such as Charles Marshall and Walter Taylor, and his postwar confidant at Lexington, the Reverend John William Jones.

These men were the nucleus of an organized effort devoted

to enhancing the reputation of Robert E. Lee. They were the movers behind the Lee Memorial Association, the Lee Monument Association, the Association of the Army of Northern Virginia, and other South-wide organizations that embellished the General's exploits. In several hundred books, articles, and orations, his devotees fashioned the image of the invincible Lee who was outnumbered but never defeated. As General John Gordon insisted, in a speech to a hall packed with Confederate veterans, "Lee was never really beaten. Lee could not be beaten."

Still, a survey of all this rhetoric of the Inner Lost Cause reveals something deeper. The arguments of political justification, chivalric conduct, and Lee's military skill were grounded on a fourth touchstone—the insistence that defeated Confederates were the *better men.*

The theme of moral superiority was the basic appeal of the former Confederate generation. The lengthy political apologies of Jefferson Davis and Alexander Stephens displayed a moral ingredient. The appeal to chivalry asserted the Christian-knight motif. Even the advocates of the "overwhelmed but undefeated" rationale often compared southern generals of exceptional character with a weaker lot of northern leaders whose only asset was the advantage of superior manpower.

Even during the war, the southern faith in moral righteousness was prominent. In 1862 the editor of the *Southern Literary Messenger* observed that a Confederate "is now, as he has always been and we trust will always be, superior to the Northern man." Dixie people held to this belief, even during harder times. In early 1865 an Atlanta editor characterized northerners as "a swindling race" who fought the Confederacy only because of "their insatiable desire for filthy lucre."

Surrender only intensified the southern desire to prove themselves the better people. Edward Pollard proclaimed that northern folk were burdened with "a sneaking sense of inferiority," and a writer in the Lost Cause magazine, *The Land We Love*, described the Union victors as a hybrid of "Yankees and negroes, Germans and Irish." The masthead of *The Land We Love* summarized the rationale, stating that "No nation rose so white and fair, Or fell so pure of crimes" as did the Confederacy. It was no accident that the phrase was lifted from verses dedicated to General Robert E. Lee. By the 1880s his character, lineage, and military fame had become the absolute rationale of the Inner Lost Cause. Lee was the epitome of the belief that a finer society had lost the war, and his virtues were held up as evidence that might does not always produce right.

The praise of Lee's character by orators and writers of the Reconstruction South would fill volumes. To Jefferson Davis, Lee's life was "a high model for the imitation of generations yet unborn." Senator Ben Hill of Georgia described him as "a public officer without vices; a private citizen without wrong . . . a man without guile," and the editor of the *Southern Magazine* labeled the General as "the noblest type of manhood that this age has produced."

More vital to an understanding of the real importance of such symbolism was an 1876 article on Lee's character written by one of his former officers, Captain John Chamberlayne. To Chamberlayne, Lee was "so blameless as might become a Saint . . . so simple as might become the little children 'of whom is the kingdom of Heaven.'"

Here was an expression of the religious-moral symbolism that underscored the Lost Cause mentality. In effect, Lee became the image of the perfect man, who was a Christ-symbol for a defeated Confederacy. Some explanation of this type was required to satisfy the basic nature of southern piety. When the expected deliverance did not come in the war, the gnawing question was how could so fine a society, guided by Jehovah, be reduced to ashes?

What resulted was an appeal by the Lost Cause advocates to the Christian interpretation of history. Man was an instrument of Divine Providence, and often must endure travail as part of God's discipline. A catastrophe did not prove lack of merit, but only demonstrated God's providence at work. Thus success proved nothing about right and wrong. After all, if Christ had his Gethsemane, Lee endured Appomattox.

There were two levels to the metaphor. Postwar Dixie writers described Lee as the stainless human and military leader. They spoke of his devotion to his mother, his love for his children, and even his kindness to animals. Steadily Lee became less human and more a saintly figure who lacked the flaws of mortals.

He became even more than a saint. The vital part of this moral rationale was the metaphor that compared Robert E. Lee to Christ. Early biographies, magazine articles, and orations stressed the likeness between the two men. Lee's decision made in 1861 at Arlington was compared to Christ's three temptations in the wilderness. One writer saw Lee's travail in this fateful decision to resign from the United States Army as comparable to Jesus at the Last Supper. Other authors and orators saw in Lee's postwar acceptance of defeat a reincarnation of Christ's walk to Calvary. Here were two men without blemish who bore without murmur the burdens of their people.

This last facet of the Lee-Christ metaphor appeared most frequently. Like Jesus, Robert E. Lee became the sacrificial lamb without blemish, given up as a sacrifice for his people. Perhaps Lee's Christ symbolism has held considerable importance in southern theology. Given the nature of southern piety, Lee's deification may show that his fellow Confederates saw him as the sacrificial lamb, who died for their own sins—whether slavery, secession, or the war. More than one writer and orator came close to expressing this openly.

When Edward Valentine's famous recumbent figure of Lee was unveiled at Lexington, Virginia, in the 1880s, the principal speaker, John Daniel, invoked this symbolism. Lee perished in 1870 because he bore the South's problems. Daniel stated, "The shoulders began to stoop as if under a growing burden. . . . What he suffered his lips have never spoken." To Daniel, Robert E. Lee's decision in 1861 was comparable to "the agony and bloody sweat of Gethsemane, and to the Cross of Calvary beyond." Even an author of popular southern children's books in the era, Mary Williamson, used this symbolism. Mrs. Williamson's Lee was Christ incarnate. Lee exuded "absolute purity." Indeed, "perhaps no man ever lived that was so great, so good and so unselfish." The symbolism of the Cross was present in Lee's last hours, for the author speculated that "the strain and hardships of the war, with sorrow for the Lost Cause," produced the tragedy, resulted in his death.

There was but one flaw in this portrayal of Lee as the superhuman. It was not difficult to describe Lee as the heir to a rich tradition of the Revolutionary era, the chivalric soldier and the man of sterling character. The only impediment to the absolute humanistic image of Lee as knight, Christian, and soldier was *Gettysburg*, which threatened his invincible stature.

One doubts if southerners have ever made peace with Gettysburg. For the neoclassical Dixie mind, wedded to absolutes, the battle has remained a blend of past and present, the nagging might-have-been of a metahistorical situation. What if "Stonewall" Jackson had lived to march with Lee to Pennsylvania? What if General Richard Ewell had fought harder on July 1 to seize the critical Culp's Hill sector? Could General James Longstreet's assault against the Union left wing have succeeded on July 2, and might the Pickett-Pettigrew attack on July 3 have succeeded?

For southerners, Gettysburg has always remained, as *Saturday Review of Literature* editor Bernard DeVoto described decades ago, that "Everlasting If," which still kindles a lingering passion in Dixie blood. Those three days in Pennsylvania have become for the South a combination of balm, metaphor, and rationale, the high-water mark that could have altered the course of American history. It is almost an article of faith for southerners to believe in the element of chance at Gettysburg, a battle that the poet Allen Tate observed "has offered greater temptations to IFS and MIGHT-HAVE-BEENS than any other battle fought on this continent." Gettysburg is the ultimate symbol of the South's nearness to the elusive goal of success. It was the core of William Faulkner's famous passage in *Intruder in the Dust*, when attorney Gavin Stevens explained to his young nephew that for every southern lad, it will always be the afternoon of July 3, when George Pickett readied his division near Emmitsburg Road. Faulkner captured the southerner's grasp of linear time, of past irrevocably merged into present. It is a southern youth's birthright to believe that Gettysburg has not happened yet. "Stonewall" Jackson will rise, unharmed, from the road near Chancellorsville and join Robert E. Lee in Pennsylvania, and that awful, cataclysmic event at Gettysburg that brought Dixie to her knees still can somehow be avoided.

And yet, the ifs and might-have-beens of Gettysburg do not explain totally why defeat has made southerners uneasy since Appomattox. Fortunes of war proved wily and fickle on other battlefields where chance could have altered events. Where would Ulysses Grant's reputation have been if his army had been destroyed in the Rebel surprise attack at Shiloh? What if Robert E. Lee had counterattacked at Fredericksburg in 1862, when the shattered Union army lay astride the Rappahannock River? And if "Stonewall" Jackson had not been shot down at Chancellorsville, would the Federal army have been driven into the same river? All of the fates were not gathered at Gettysburg.

Important here is that the outcome of Gettysburg threatened the entire rationale of the Inner Lost Cause. It was the only obvious battlefield defeat suffered by Robert E. Lee. Gettysburg marred the Lee image of perfection, which was the cornerstone of the Inner Lost Cause. The stainless man and the chivalrous knight must be also the impeccable warrior. The leading figure in the Lost Cause imagery was defeated in *the* battle that even the earliest historians on both sides described as decisive.

Worse, for almost a decade after Appomattox, the major war historians, southern and otherwise, assigned to Lee the principal blame for the loss at Gettysburg. Edward Pollard, John Esten Cooke, James McCabe, and other Confederate historians provided accounts that agreed basically with northern writers such as William Swinton and foreign observers. Although accounts varied in detail, the basic nonpartisan version of Confederate loss at Gettysburg was an indictment of Lee. On July 1 Lee mishandled Richard Ewell's corps, losing an opportunity to seize the Culp's Hill region and force a Federal retreat. On July 2 and 3 an overconfident Lee disregarded the wiser counsel of General Longstreet, and ordered instead suicidal attacks against the Union line on Cemetery Ridge.

When Lee died in 1870, the consensus of historians still ran against him on the Gettysburg question. He did not live to know—and would have protested—that within a single decade, the responsibility for defeat was shifted almost completely to his corps leader, General James Longstreet.

Longstreet's fate as the scapegoat of the Lost Cause is so well known that no full explanation is required here. It is a historiographical puzzle, involving a total "rewriting" of the Gettysburg saga by former Confederates. During the 1870s, the organization and literary power of the developing Lost Cause mentality centered in the old war theater of the Army of Northern Virginia.

The most powerful Lost Cause magazines and organizations

existed here. Here was the South's principal historical organization, the Southern Historical Society, which was controlled by Lee devotees such as Jubal Early, John William Jones, and Fitzhugh Lee. The group issued the Society's *Papers*, the most influential magazine in the South for decades. Alfred Bledsoe's Baltimore-based *Southern Review* echoed his own belief that Robert E. Lee embodied the "purity, stability and greatness" of Dixie. The most powerful veterans' group in the South, the Association of the Army of Northern Virginia, was dominated by members of this same body of admirers, including Lee's son "Rooney" and his nephew, Fitzhugh Lee. Other regional groups maintained headquarters in Virginia, including the large Lee Memorial and Lee Monument associations.

These people were the core of the Inner Lost Cause, and one scarcely can exaggerate their influence on Confederate letters in the nineteenth century. Nor can one understate their fervor to preserve Robert E. Lee as the absolute Lost Cause symbol. They viewed themselves as trustees and protectors of Lee's reputation, with a mission to prove General John Gordon's exhortation that "Lee was never really beaten. Lee could not be beaten."

Possessed of such organization and zeal, the artists of the Inner Lost Cause reshaped the southern version of Gettysburg. The confusing, bitter wrangle of the 1870s between Longstreet and a score of writers is beyond this discussion. It is enough to say that under the direction of such prominent Confederate authors as Jubal Early and John William Jones, all of the weaponry of the Lost Cause was turned against Longstreet. He was assailed in dozens of articles in the *Southern Historical Society Papers* and other war magazines, and was damned in an outpouring of oratory at veterans' meetings, Lee memorial services, and elsewhere.

The story of Gettysburg had changed drastically by the 1880s. The basic Confederate version no longer criticized Lee's overall direction of the battle. Nor were Richard Ewell and his subordinate Jubal Early blamed for any lack of determination in the Culp's Hill sector on July 1. Longstreet was now the absolute malefactor because of his alleged slowness in executing Lee's attack plans on July 2. Early and former general William Nelson Pendleton even developed a tale that Longstreet had specific orders to attack that day at sunrise. Although they despised Longstreet, several of Lee's former staff members, including Lost Cause authors Charles Marshall and Walter Taylor, admitted that such an order was a fantasy. Nevertheless, "Longstreet's slowness at Gettysburg" henceforth was the basic southern explanation for defeat.

With an intense degree of hatred, the Lost Cause authors rode Longstreet unmercifully for decades. He became an object of hatred for that generation of Confederate writers. General Richard Taylor, in his *Destruction and Reconstruction*, likened Lee and Longstreet to the biblical Balaam and his ass. Colonel Charles Marshall, Lee's former aide, vowed that the Georgian "must make amends for his grevious [sic] faults," while Colonel Walter Taylor insisted that "give General Longstreet rope enough and he will soon hang himself." John William Jones declared to his comrade Jubal Early, "I am anxious for you to slice up what is left of Longstreet." Even in the last year of Longstreet's life, as he was dying from cancer, his old colleague from Lee's army, General John Gordon, berated his fellow Georgian in his *Reminiscences of the Civil War*.

In the eyes of the leaders of the Inner Lost Cause, James Longstreet had committed three cardinal sins. In all three matters, he was extremely vulnerable. They—and many other southerners—never forgave him for joining the Republican ranks during Reconstruction, and becoming active in that party's fortunes first in Louisiana and later in Georgia. Longstreet himself knew that some regarded him as a traitor. In 1867, even before becoming active in postwar politics, he had published some letters in the New Orleans *Times* advising southerners to accept the dictates of the Radical Republican Congress. Longstreet recalled later that from that day old war comrades refused to speak to him.

A second transgression was Longstreet's supposed disobedience of orders at Gettysburg. In 1872, when Early fired the first salvo in an address at Washington and Lee University, already Longstreet was the scapegoat. Early contended that if Longstreet had carried out Lee's orders, "a decisive victory would have been obtained, which perhaps would have secured our independence." As time passed, the *perhaps* vanished from the vocabulary of the Inner Lost Cause. Amid the hunger to pull some semblance of victory from the ashes of total defeat, Gettysburg became the great denouement, where the fate of the South was decided in a few hours by Longstreet's alleged stubborn behavior.

Here Longstreet made himself vulnerable in his first postwar remarks about the battle. William Swinton's *Campaigns of the Army of the Potomac* was considered the most authoritative source on Gettysburg in the late 1860s. Swinton documented "a full and free conversation" with Longstreet in late 1865, in which the General admitted that he and Lee had disagreed strongly on the decision to attack at Gettysburg. In this initial memoir, Longstreet established himself as the dissident and then proceeded to catalog for Swinton the several errors committed by Lee in the Pennsylvania campaign.

Here was the basic reason for James Longstreet's image as the wrongdoer. Not once, but on numerous occasions, the Georgian committed the unforgivable sin in the era of the Inner Lost Cause; he criticized the reputation of Robert E. Lee. As the Gettysburg controversy raged through the 1870s and thereafter, Longstreet defended his reputation in magazine articles, letters to newspapers, and eventually the memoir, *From Manassas to Appomattox*. Every defense brought renewed critiques of Lee's military reputation.

Longstreet blundered into the literary fray as he would fight a battle, with scant finesse but a stubborn tenacity. He was a fighter, not a thinker, and did not sense the emotional mood of the Confederate generation. Certainly Longstreet was an ambitious man, and the evidence supports the theory that during the war he desired his own army command. There is documentation, for example, that he intrigued in 1863 to obtain command of the Confederate army on the western front.

Still, he was a paradox, as are most southerners, and his ability to intrigue was matched by a blunt, almost naïve honesty. Angry and desperate to defend himself, Longstreet repeatedly charged into the dispute, armed with disparaging comments about Lee's conduct at Gettysburg. He seemed unaware that the essence of the Inner Lost Cause was the canonization of Lee as the invincible Confederate symbol. Because Longstreet did not perceive this, his own reputation suffered badly, and his postwar image in the South is filled with irony. He served the Rebel cause from Bull Run to the last day of Appomattox and ended his career as the respected senior corps leader of Lee's Army of Northern Virginia.

Earlier, in 1862–1863, Lee, "Stonewall" Jackson, and Longstreet comprised that formidable triumvirate of the Confederate army. There was Lee the planner, Jackson the bold executor of rapid movements, and Longstreet as the dogged, reliable hammer of the Virginia army.

Jackson died in 1863, covered with glory, as a Confederate hero. Seven years later Lee died in Lexington, cognizant of his popularity but probably unaware of the potential impact of his hero symbolism.

Longstreet survived until 1903, when he died after almost four decades of pain from a wound received in the Wilderness encounter. Statues to the memories of Jackson and Lee sprouted along Richmond's Monument Avenue and elsewhere on the southern landscape, but no courthouse or battlefield shaft was raised in honor of Longstreet. The funeral ceremonies for Jackson and Lee were massive, traumatic outpourings of grief. When Longstreet died, deaf and nearly blind from cancer, a Savannah chapter of the United Daughters of the Confederacy voted not to send flowers to the funeral, and a North Carolina group of Confederate veterans chose not to send condolences to the family. At the same time, however, editorials in southern newspapers suggested that it was time to forgive James Longstreet.

Forgive him for what? Certainly Longstreet's postwar espousal of the Republican faith had caused wide resentment among his old war comrades. As well, because of the revisionism produced by the Inner Lost Cause artists, other southerners honestly believed that Longstreet was responsible for Gettysburg's loss. His role of the uncooperative and unyielding subordinate did render him vulnerable to the criticisms of writers. But Longstreet's old artillery leader, General Porter Alexander, later surmised that Longstreet's greatest error was to criticize Lee.

The Confederate sense of estrangement was one prime factor in the fashioning of Robert E. Lee as the absolute Confederate symbol. Stainless in conduct and invincible in generalship, Lee's image could prove that the righteous sometimes do not prevail. As well, Longstreet may have come to represent the anti-Christ within the southern trinity. Modern scholars should not take such symbolism too far, but it appears that Longstreet did symbolize evil to some of his old war comrades. To them he became the traitor Republican, the Judas who attempted to mar Lee's reputation, and one whose misconduct at Gettysburg snatched away victory in the Confederacy's hour of destiny.

The first postwar generation of southern writers accomplished much. During the first decade of the twentieth century, the angry, noncompromising mentality of the Inner Lost Cause had dwindled to a few aged, angry voices. In less than four decades, General Robert E. Lee had been enshrined as the prime hero symbol of the Confederacy. Reputations of other southern war figures had been altered, if not destroyed. Gettysburg had become the eternal southern moment, and the saga of the battle had been rewritten.

There was something else. The architects of the Inner Lost Cause had revealed the importance of that lasting bond between Confederate memory and southern piety.

Chapter Two

HOW VIRGINIA WON THE CIVIL WAR

"We Virginians," wrote the distinguished author and journalist Virginius Dabney, "modestly admit our superiority to citizens of all other American states." In one sentence, Dabney described the character of the Old Dominion that has intrigued writers for generations.

The attempt to explain to outsiders peculiarities of the Virginia tradition has taxed the efforts of some of the best writers of the commonwealth. After the Civil War, John Esten Cooke attacked the problem in his *Virginia: A History of the People.* It was easy for Cooke to describe the praiseworthy habits of his fellow Virginians, to speak of their courtesy, hospitality, and close-knit family traditions. Why these attributes were not shared by other southerners—and all Americans—was more difficult to explain. Cooke tried gamely to describe the unique "ingrained" qualities of the Virginia character; he suggested that the credo of Virginians was "to love one's native soil and to cherish the home traditions which give character to a race."

The Virginia novelist and biographer Thomas Nelson Page exhibited less reserve. His address at the 1907 Jamestown tricentennial exhibition described the special nature of Virginia in near-theological reasoning. The commonwealth was a special place touched by the Almighty, because "it has been well said that God acts through his prepared agencies, and that He prepared Virginia to place the seal of His favor on." To

Page, Jamestown was the "holy ground" from whence went forth "the streams which have made the great main of American life."

Years later, in the era of the southern renascence, the famous biographer of Robert E. Lee, Douglas Southall Freeman, wrote and spoke much about the special qualities of the Virginia tradition. Freeman believed strongly, as he described in a 1925 address in Richmond, that "Virginia is different," and that Lee's Army of Northern Virginia constituted an "Army of Gentlemen." Freeman praised often what he considered the special character of his state. In 1919 he addressed the Virginia General Assembly on the three-hundredth anniversary of the organization of the House of Burgesses, and boasted that Virginia "carried the standard of advanced free government on the continent." To Freeman, the reasons for the superiority of Virginians were simple ones. He explained in a 1935 speech at Lee's ancestral home of Stratford that the greatness of Virginia rested in a mixture of good breeding and the gentlemanly qualities of the noblesse oblige.

Still, Cooke, Page, and Dr. Freeman did not describe the Virginia tradition in the succinct manner of Virginius Dabney. It remains, as Dabney wrote, that Virginians "modestly admit our superiority" to other American mortals.

There was much truth in an 1871 letter written by Professor Charles Venable of the University of Virginia to his old war comrade, General Jubal Early. Venable, a long-time member of the personal staff of Robert E. Lee, commented upon the attitude that he and other Virginia soldiers held during the war. He observed, "We lived in an atmosphere of victory and were unconscious of the . . . disasters which were befalling us in almost every other part of the Confederacy."

The wartime and postwar mentality of Virginians reflected the inbred conceit that characterized citizens of the Dominion from colonial times. It was part of a Virginian's heritage to believe that his state was the Cradle of Democracy. It was not un-usual when Thomas Nelson Page spoke in his very popular work, *The Old Dominion*, of how Virginia was the "Birthplace of the American people," and observed, "It was by no mere ac-cident that Washington, Jefferson, Madison, Marshall, Henry, Mason and their like came from Tidewater and Piedmont Vir-ginia. They were the proper product of her distinctive Civiliza-tion." Nor was it unusual for George Cary Eggleston to observe that "The old life of the Old Dominion is . . . one so different from anything that exists anywhere," or for his cohort Sara Pryor to reminisce about an 1861 reception in Washington where her rooms were filled "with Virginians and Southerners mainly, but with some northern friends as well, for Virginia was not yet classed."

They were in a class of their own before, during, and after the war. It was the Richmond *Whig* in April of 1861 that published a verse titled "Virginia's Call to Arms," which depicted the cur-rent sectional tragedy in part as a result of an ungrateful North unmindful of Virginia's primary role in creating a United States. Only three days earlier, an editorial in the *Whig* had re-minded all that Virginia "has done more than any other State to create the Union—she had given intellect and money and a rich dowery in her Northwestern territory." Now the poet observed:

> I gave them broad dominions,
> I gave them liberty,
> And now the ungrateful minions,
> Have turned to fetter me.

In war and peace, clearly Virginians wanted to be first. They sought the best of both worlds—to be the sorrowful, reluc-tant lovers of Union who were dragooned into the secessionist camp. At the same time, they claimed to be the leaders of that war against the Old Flag. Eggleston observed that without Virginia's "pluck and pith there could have been no war at all worth writing or talking about." Page echoed this sentiment in a description of Richmond in *The Old Dominion*: "From here the Southern side of the war was fought. To seize Richmond the armies and energies of the North were directed, and for it they strove. While it stood the Confederacy stood, and it fell only when the South was exhausted."

The relationship between such expressions of Virginia pride and the artistry of the Lost Cause has never been given enough serious consideration. In fact, one could make a strong argument that the principal driving force behind the entire Lost Cause mentality came from Virginia. Virginia authors denied repeatedly for generations that the people of the Commonwealth shared the same commitment to secession and slavery that characterized the remainder of the South. From Appomattox until well into the twentieth century, Virginia authors fashioned an image of how an unwilling Old Dominion was forced into the Civil War by the hotheads of sister states in Dixie. Paradoxically, however, if one examines the literary and commemorative organization of the Lost Cause mentality, the power structure rested in Virginia.

Certainly the mentality that generated the Confederate writings of the Inner Lost Cause was shared by other southerners. In the Reconstruction era and later, veterans' organizations and local Confederate memorial associations existed throughout the South. Also, former politicians and Rebel officers wrote their memoirs in Georgia and Louisiana as well as in Virginia.

The same could be said for the architects of the later National Lost Cause. Those southern authors who wrote for the northern market in the last decades of the nineteenth century, and into the period before World War I, were not all Virginians. James Lane Allen wrote of the Cumberland Mountains of Kentucky, George Washington Cable portrayed the antebellum life of Louisiana Creoles, and Mary Chesnut's posthumous *Diary from Dixie* was the work of a South Carolinian. It was the Georgia journalist Joel Chandler Harris who helped to popularize the imagery of the contented plantation slave.

Still, there is strong evidence that the greatest participant in both Lost Cause movements, Inner and National, was Virginia. One is struck especially by the irony of Virginia dominance of the Inner Lost Cause. Although Virginia authors persistently denied their state's devotion to the underlying factors that produced secession, the Confederacy, and the war, no one worked harder to perpetuate the Confederate memory. For decades after Appomattox, the most influential war publication in the South was the *Southern Historical Society Papers*; even the *New England Historical Register* noted that "no library, public, or private, which pretends to historic fullness, *Can Afford to Be Without These Volumes.*" The Southern Historical Society, organized first at New Orleans in 1869, was revamped at White Sulphur Springs in 1873. Under the new order, the society, allegedly a South-wide body, was squarely under the control of the Old Dominion. All members of the ruling executive committee were required to be Virginia residents, and the group's headquarters were in Richmond. For years the society's *Papers* was under the control of veterans of Robert E. Lee's army such as John William Jones, Jubal Early, and Robert Brock. Consequently, for some four decades after its first publication in 1876, the *Papers* was devoted primarily to Virginia's role in the Civil War. The 1877 volume, for example, contained forty-four articles on the Virginia war theater and only five on the remainder of the Confederacy.

The pattern was evident in other activities of the Inner Lost Cause. The Lee Monument Association and Lee Memorial Association were large organizations with professional fundraising agents and skillful public relations efforts designed to extol the virtues of General Lee and the Army of Northern Virginia. The Confederate Memorial Association (1896) was organized in Atlanta to build a Valhalla of Confederate heroes. Financed South-wide and intended as a memorial for all Rebels, the project's directors gave way to Virginia demands, and the edifice, described by one speaker as "what Melrose Abby is to Scotland, Westminister to England, and the glorious Pantheon to France," was placed in Richmond. Richmond was headquarters as well for the United Daughters of the Confederacy (1895). And for fifteen years after its organization in 1889, the powerful United Confederate Veterans was headed by General John Gordon, former corps commander in the Army of Northern Virginia. Virginia did more than any former Rebel state to keep alive the memory of the Inner Lost Cause.

The same literary dominance was evident in the later nineteenth-century efforts of the National Lost Cause. From the 1880s until the First World War, Virginia authors dominated the rising tide of romanticism and reunion in southern letters. The literary input of those writers to magazines such as *Harper's*, *Lippincott's*, *Atlantic Monthly*, and *Appleton's* was awesome. Novelist John Esten Cooke published forty-nine articles in *Harper's* and *Appleton's* alone. Cooke, Thomas Nelson Page, Sara Pryor, Constance Cary Harrison, Mary McClelland, Amelie Rives, Jennie Woodville, Molly Seawell, George Cary Eggleston, and many others captured national audiences with their descriptions of the glories of Virginia's past. Captain Robert E. Lee, Jr., charmed the Bostonian Charles Francis Adams with recollections of his father's life, Mrs. George Pickett serialized her reminiscences for *Cosmopolitan*, and Constance Cary Harrison, a former Richmond belle, delighted readers with *Reminiscences Grave and Gay*.

An argument could be made that the real Lost Cause was not the South, but was Virginia. In the writings and activities of both Lost Cause movements, southern and national, Virginia writers approached the subject with passion. This remains one of the great ironies of southern letters, for many of these same people repeatedly played down Virginia's role in the secession crisis. Later, in the literature of the National Lost Cause, no group fashioned a more picturesque image of an Old South replete with mansions, noble masters, and loyal servants than did the dominant Virginians. Yet these same writers consistently asserted that Virginians did not actually approve of slavery.

More significantly, authors of both genres of Lost Cause literature designed a convincing image of themselves as nonparticipants in secession. However, these writers boasted repeatedly that Virginia led the southern war effort. Certainly they were motivated by the same general moods of bitterness, defeat, and a desire for justification that affected other southerners in their time. But the Virginians wrote under the added burden of an alchemy of lost status, injured pride, and guilt. They were obsessed with being first.

One is haunted by some remarks made by Thomas Nelson Page in his book *The Old Dominion.* In a section on great public leaders produced by the commonwealth, Page evoked the names of Washington, Jefferson, Madison, Monroe, John Marshall, Patrick Henry, Henry Clay, Robert E. Lee, and others. The comparison of this list with great public names in Virginia since the Civil War is striking. The modern observer of Virginia culture, Marshall Fishwick, suggested that from the Reconstruction years until the present age, Virginia politics have been dominated by William Mahone, Thomas Martin, James Cannon, Carter Glass, and Harry Byrd. In the long history from Thomas Jefferson to Harry Byrd, one saw the decay of Virginia's golden age of eighteenth-century aristocracy, the decline of the tobacco kingdom, and the loss of national political reputation.

For four decades after Appomattox, Virginia authors, in fiction, history, and biography, never ceased to dwell upon the glories of the Old Dominion's past. A mosaic of images became stock items in their literature—Virginia the cradle of American civilization, the leader of the American Revolution, the designer of the Constitution, and the birthplace of great American statesmen.

How could they reconcile their self-image as the creator of the Union with their role in the Confederacy? Certainly the Virginia authors of the Lost Cause desired to have it both ways—to boast of their role in making the nation and their preeminent position in the effort to rend it asunder.

It proved a difficult dilemma and was not resolved immediately. The Confederate mentality of the Inner Lost Cause did not attempt to cope with the dichotomy of this image, because their efforts were more self-directed than national in focus. Instead, the task of resolving the inconsistency was undertaken by that new bevy of writers of the National Lost Cause who rose to prominence in the 1880s. These people strove to explain the Confederate experience to the entire nation.

All of this was very new, because for almost a decade after the Civil War, the national press published little about the American past. After the horror of over 600,000 dead, 10 million wounded, and the damage to the American spirit, the nation was tired of war journalism, battle reports, and lists of draft quotas. Probably there were also feelings of guilt that prompted readers to prefer magazine and newspaper articles more attuned toward the national future. Let the past rest for a time, and speak now of iron rails across the Great Plains, the silver question, or the Grant scandals.

So the American past, and particularly the southern past, remained noticeably unexplored for almost a decade after Appomattox. War weariness, hostility toward the South, and absorption in the Industrial Revolution were reflected in the nation's press. *Harper's New Monthly Magazine*, edited by staunch New Englander George Curtis, published only articles uncomplimentary to southern culture. The classic was a shrewd appraisal of the Dixie mentality by a former Charleston resident and Federal officer, John De Forest. In 1869 De Forest enraged southerners with a biting analysis entitled "Chivalrous and Semi-Chivalrous Southrons."

Most national magazines simply ignored both the war and the South. *Harper's* and the *North American Review* scarcely mentioned either topic. Except for occasional articles on Republican corruption in the South, *Nation* avoided the subjects of Dixie and the Confederacy.

The situation changed markedly in the latter 1870s when negative and positive elements joined to engender a strong national interest in the Civil War and southern culture. The interest in the South reflected changing tastes of the new mass reading public, and also, one suspects that American journalists realized that their readers had become weary or bored with more tales of railroad building and political corruption. Thus, the same resurgence of romanticism that canonized William F. Cody and Wyatt Earp as dime novel heroes produced a new interest in the South's counterculture. Edward Judson's writings on "Buffalo Bill" and John Esten Cooke's tales of chivalric Virginians helped to satisfy a desire for escapist literature.

The two decades after the Civil War were the great age of American magazines. Some 700 were published in the year of Lee's surrender. By 1885 there were 3,300 magazines. Even these figures understate the new appetites for cheap reading matter. In that twenty years, enterprising publishers had launched almost 9,000 new periodicals. Such increases were part of a response to the reading demands of a rising middle class and a growing, more literate blue-collar work force. Within two decades after Fort Sumter, there were twenty million more potential readers in the mass literary market.

No topic eluded the demand for inexpensive reading matter. The new craze for women's magazines overwhelmed the old prewar, octavo-sized fashion drawings of *Godey's* and *Peter-*

son's. Mary Booth's *Harper's Bazaar*, first published in 1867, gained almost 100,000 readers in the next decade. In 1883 the tabloid magnate Cyrus Curtis issued his *Ladies' Home Journal and Practical Housekeeper*. Curtis' circulation list of 400,000 subscribers left *Harper's Bazaar* far behind, as did *McCall's*, the brainchild of a Scottish tailor, James McCall.

These statistics reflected a general American assertion of the right to read and underscored a literary war that existed among northeastern publishers for a quarter of a century after the Civil War. The competition was fierce, especially in those general magazines that offered a mixed diet of history, poetry, fiction, and criticism.

Shortly before the Civil War, the public market was dominated by only three periodicals. In 1850 the Harper brothers had published *Harper's New Monthly Magazine* as competition for the older *North American Review*. Seven years later *Atlantic Monthly* joined the competition as Boston's contribution to "literature, art and politics." The monopoly of the trio was short-lived. *Nation*, with the vigorous editorship of E. L. Godkin, entered the market in 1865 and used the talents of such writers as Henry James and Francis Parkman. A year later *Galaxy* joined the fight with a stable of writers that included Mark Twain. In 1868 the powerful *Lippincott's Magazine* appeared, and in 1869 the subscription lists were spread thinner by the introduction of *Appleton's Journal of Literature, Science and Art*, which was illustrated with woodcuts by Winslow Homer and offered serialized fiction by Victor Hugo. Then in 1870 the rival house of Scribner's countered with the most powerful middle-class journal of the era. Circulation soared under the crusading, anticorruption editor, Dr. Josiah Holland. *Scribner's Monthly* became the first important northern magazine to publish the writings of promising southern writers such as Joel Chandler Harris and Thomas Nelson Page.

There were other factors that turned national attention toward southern culture. Never before, or perhaps since, has the nation seemed so aware of its time and place, of the absolute dichotomy between the old and new. Americans have always been conscious of the marking of time; it was a predictable trait for a young nation that measured its age in decades rather than centuries. Later the optimism mixed with nostalgia would be seen in the 1907 tricentennial of the founding of Jamestown, the 1913 "long encampment" of Gettysburg's fiftieth anniversary, the 1932 bicentennial of George Washington's birthday, the Civil War centennial, and others. However, the 1876 centennial of the Declaration of Independence marked a watershed in the country's history between the traditional agrarian way of life and the modern industrial society. The national mood was indeed almost schizophrenic. The Industrial Revolution had created a sharp conflict between old values and a rising urban, industrial order. Institutional religion was challenged by the growing popular acceptance of the social gospel, and the established social fabric, reinforced by Anglo-Saxon institutions, was threatened by the new immigration from eastern and southern Europe. Pride in country was offset by bewilderment at the rapidly changing tenor of an industrial society and by disillusionment with political corruption and the enduring sores of Reconstruction.

The contradictions between the old and the new were very evident at the extravagant 1876 centennial exposition at Philadelphia. There were displays of modern railway cars, hydraulic rams, and machines that produced straight pins. In the same buildings were exhibits of George Washington memorabilia and Ben Franklin's hand printing press.

The Philadelphia exposition was a lavish display of a nation at cross currents with its own consciousness, between the old and the new, and between fear of the future and faith in progress. Like specters from the past, Jesse and Frank James rode in 1876 to the famous Northfield, Minnesota bank robbery, but paused along the way to watch a National League baseball game in Minneapolis–St. Paul. Colonel George Armstrong Custer and several companies of cavalrymen were annihilated by the Dakota Sioux, in a year when northern tourists began flocking to vacation resorts in Florida.

Above all, there was the memory of the Civil War. The war was a national catastrophe of a degree never experienced before or since. The death toll, probably 620,000, surpassed American casualties in all other wars combined, from the Revolutionary War to Korea. Then there were the 10 million cases of wounds and disease—the amputees, endless cases of battle fatigue, and the men who never recovered from wartime ravages of dysentery, typhoid, venereal disease, and other maladies.

The exuberance of Yankee victory was dimmed by the gnawing question of why the American Dream had failed so badly, of how the model for oppressed mankind had come to such a force of arms. Meanwhile, the South's ability to lay aside sectional bitterness was hampered by the reality of defeat and the abstraction of why a cause believed to be so righteous could fail so miserably.

Still, the editor of *Scribner's Monthly*, Dr. Josiah Holland, urged that the centennial should choose national reunion as its prime objective. And in the great July 4 parade at the Philadelphia exposition, the centennial legion was led by General Henry Heth of Virginia. Thirteen years earlier, Harry Heth had marched on Pennsylvania as a division commander in the Army of Northern Virginia. His appearance at Philadelphia was no less symbolic than that of Richard Henry Lee II. Lee, cousin of the famed Rebel general who sought to capture Philadelphia in 1863, read the Declaration of Independence to an enthusiastic crowd.

The prominence of these former Confederates in the Philadelphia commemoration had far more significance than a symbolic exercise of future national reunion. Changing public tastes in the printed media, the new concern with the nation's past, the centennial—all combined to produce a strong interest in southern culture.

The changes had been evident in 1873, when the new *Scribner's Monthly* printed its well-known Great South series, which was later expanded in a highly successful book. Editor Roswell Smith sensed that a national reading public was curious about its defeated foe. He dispatched the New England journalist Edward King on a 25,000-mile tour of the old Confederacy, which produced fifteen articles on southern culture. The 1873–1874 Great South articles provided a first real look at what had been *terra incognita* for northern readers. King described the richness of the culture of the South—the Shenandoah Valley, the Elizabethan culture of the Unaka Mountains of Tennessee, Acadian Louisiana, old Charleston, and elsewhere.

The Great South series capitalized upon a changing national mood, and, predictably, its success produced imitations in other magazines. *Harper's* announced its New South series in 1874, and *Atlantic Monthly* began featuring an eleven-part Studies of the South written by a former Federal officer, Jonathan Harrison, and another series of travel accounts of southern culture by the Connecticut journalist, Charles Dudley Warner.

More important, *Scribner's* series was the vanguard of that long enchantment of northern magazines and newspapers with southern culture. The Great South articles were less pioneer efforts than the fait accompli. For whatever reason—national boredom, the emotional appeal of the centennial, curiosity about a defeated foe's culture—the South and its unique life style became a predominant theme of northern journalism by the late 1870s. Shortly before the centennial celebration, a huge outpouring of articles in newspapers and magazines displayed a new fascination with the South's culture.

The local color movement in the nation's literature supposedly embraced all sections of the nation and all varieties of the culture of the old Confederacy. The frail, well-to-do Mary Noailles Murfree, who wrote under the pseudonym Charles Egbert Craddock, cultivated a national audience with her stories of life in the Tennessee mountains. The former Union officer and adopted North Carolinian, Albion Tourgée, wrote romantic novels of the Reconstruction South such as *A Fool's Errand.*

Meanwhile a culture-conscious nation "discovered" a former Confederate soldier, George Washington Cable. Cable had been employed in a New Orleans warehouse when he met Edward King, who had come to Louisiana in search of material for the Great South series. King recognized the literary talents of Cable, who soon furnished *Scribner's Monthly* with tales of Louisiana culture. Soon came Cable's 1879 collection of stories, *Old Creole Days,* and popular novels such as *The Grandissimes.*

What is important here is that the local color movement of the 1870s and 1880s was dominated by Virginia writers and topics. That *Atlantic Monthly* within two years published eleven articles on Thomas Jefferson prior to the centennial was not unusual. The centennial naturally focused upon the colonial heritage of Virginia, just as a new era of romanticism in American literature would be attracted to the image of a cavalier society. In turn, Virginia was the unquestioned center of a literary, impoverished South. No other Rebel state could muster such an array of literary talent—John Esten Cooke, Edward Pollard, George Bagby, Thomas Nelson Page, Margaret Preston, Jennie Stabler, George Cary Eggleston, and many others.

Lippincott's featured Edward Pollard's account of wartime experiences in Richmond, and several articles on Virginia life by John Williamson Palmer, author of the popular wartime Rebel song, "Stonewall Jackson's Way." Jennie Stabler wrote nine articles on Virginia life, such as "How Ham Was Cured," and Mary McClelland, relative of the more famous Virginia writer Thomas Nelson Page, published several entire novels in *Lippincott's* that described plantation life in the Old Dominion. *Scribner's* fought back with its own new-found stable of Virginia authors. Thomas Nelson Page made his national debut with pieces such as "Uncle Gab's White Folks," while novelist John Esten Cooke charmed readers with accounts of colonial and antebellum Virginia culture. The vivacious Constance Cary Harrison first appeared before a national reading audience with two popular articles, "A Little Centennial Lady" and "My Lord Fairfax of Virginia." Meanwhile illustrator Allen Redwood, a veteran of "Stonewall" Jackson's campaigns, wrote articles on his war experiences, and other Virginia writers, such as John Thompson, Thomas Dunn English, Armistead Gordon, and Margaret Preston, published essays and poetry.

Harper's New Monthly editors observed the success of these purveyors of Virginia romanticism and soon joined the competition. John Esten Cooke was wooed away from *Scribner's* to produce some of his finest short pieces, such as "Unc' Edinburg's Drowndin'" and "Ole 'Stracted." Cooke was viewed as valuable property during the era of the 1876 centennial, and he responded by writing almost a dozen articles that eulogized antebellum Virginia's culture or praised the colonial era. Other local writers graced the pages of *Harper's*. Frederick Daniel described Revolutionary Virginia in articles entitled "In an Old Virginia Town" and "A Visit to a Colonial Estate."

The emphasis on Virginia in national magazines during the decade after Appomattox appears almost incredible. The impact of the 1876 centennial, curiosity about a defeated enemy, and American romantic literary tastes proved to be a powerful combination. Few major periodicals failed to capitalize upon the peculiar charm of Virginia's culture. For example, *Atlantic Monthly* between 1870 and 1873 produced eleven articles on Thomas Jefferson. *Century Illustrated Magazine*, the successor to the older *Scribner's Monthly* in the 1880s, joined the national interest in Virginia lore. A Maryland engineer and painter, Francis Hopkinson Smith, was highly successful with his serialized novel, *Colonel Carter of Cartersville*, the traditional narrative of the aged planter and his faithful black servant. Thomas Nelson Page moved to the *Century* staff and furnished several articles published later in his influential book, *In Old Virginia*, such as "Marse Chan" and "Meh Lady: A Story of the War."

The undisputed leader of this legion of Virginia romantics was John Esten Cooke. Cooke's prewar novels, such as *Leather Stocking and Silk* (1854) and *The Virginia Comedians* (1854), established him as the foremost Virginia romantic novelist of the era. During the war, in numerous articles and several books, Cooke proved to be a superb literary opportunist well attuned to the changing tastes of his reading public. In mid-war when the career of "Stonewall" Jackson overshadowed even that of Robert E. Lee, Cooke concentrated upon Jackson's career. While serving in the Army of Northern Virginia, Cooke supplemented his officer's pay by working as a free-lance correspondent for such popular Dixie periodicals as the *Southern Illustrated News* and the *Southern Literary Messenger*.

His first biography of Jackson was published in serial form in early 1863. "Stonewall Jackson and the Old Stonewall Brigade" heaped praise on Jackson, described by Cooke as the "Greatest of Generals," and one than whom "no soldier of the war has been more uniformly successful in his undertakings."

After Jackson's death in the late spring of 1863, Cooke joined the rush of biographers who sought to capitalize upon the career of the popular Confederate leader. Scarcely two weeks after Jackson fell at Chancellorsville, the *Southern Illustrated News* began advertising Cooke's future publication, *The Life of Stonewall Jackson*. Cooke's penchant for recognizing a popular subject was obvious. Jackson died in early May; by August,

Richmond steam presses were producing Cooke's 300-page eulogy, which sold 3,000 copies on the day it was issued and was later pirated by New York and London publishers.

It is not surprising that in 1871 Appleton and Company issued Cooke's *A Life of Gen. Robert E. Lee,* less than a year after the General's death. Lee by the 1870s was becoming the ultimate symbol and rationale of the Lost Cause. While Cooke's biography contained elements that displeased avid Lee cultists, such as continuing praise of "Stonewall" Jackson, the biography was a compendium of those traits that eventually were used to characterize the image of Robert E. Lee. The author described the General's impeccable character, Anglo-Saxon ancestry, and family contributions to the Revolutionary experience.

John Esten Cooke was a prodigious, facile writer who combined literary talent, devotion to the Virginia mystique, and a pragmatic approach to the fickle appetites of his reading public. Here was Cooke's important contribution to the Lost Cause rationale. He obviously sensed the growing neoromanticism in American letters of the seventies and capitalized upon themes of the idyllic nature of plantation life in Virginia, devoted black servants, and cavaliers in Rebel uniforms who raged larger than life.

Cooke rarely deviated from this formula. He published scores of articles in magazines and newspapers such as *Appleton's Journal, Harper's New Monthly*, the Philadelphia *Times*, and the Detroit *Free Press*. A typical Cooke article was his 1876 *Harper's* contribution, "Virginia in the Revolution." In describing the slave culture of colonial Virginia, Cooke depicted the bond servant as "well fed, and rarely overtaxed; generally had his own patch of ground . . . was a merry, jovial, musical being, and when his day's work was over, played his banjo in front of his cabin, and laughed and jested and danced by the light of the moon." For readers of a Baltimore newspaper, Confederate hero Turner Ashby was a "knightly figure . . . the perfect flower of chivalry and honor," and for readers of the Philadelphia *Times*, General J. E. B. Stuart was one who "stood out from the great war canvas like a prominent figure in some painting. . . . He always struck men as a sort of knight errant of the middle ages." These same themes were plied in a number of successful books. Cooke's *Surry of Eagle's Nest* (1866), the first important Civil War novel, glorified the cavalier image of Robert E. Lee's Army of Northern Virginia. In 1867 Cooke issued his war reminiscences, *Wearing of the Gray*. Dedicated to his beloved J. E. B. Stuart, "Flower of Cavaliers," the book was a romantic saga of battles in the Commonwealth. In 1869–1870, the indefatigable Cooke followed with three romantic novels on Virginia in the war—*Hilt to Hilt; Mohun: Or the Last Days of Lee and His Paladins;* and *Hammer and Rapier.*

It is important to remember that John Esten Cooke was not writing for the Confederate veteran. In fact, sometimes his fellow former Rebels even became irritated at his work. For example, his 1871 biography of Lee was disliked by the more devoted Lee cultists. Professor Charles Venable of the University of Virginia, a former member of the General's staff, described the book as "deplorable." Another admirer, Colonel William Allan, labeled Cooke as one of "a crop of vultures . . . meddling with the history of our cause."

Cooke was not disinterested in "our cause," but sensed that he could down several birds with one proverbial stone—gain profit from his literary ventures, praise his beloved Virginia before a national audience, and at the same time help to justify the Confederate experience.

Here was Cooke's contribution to the winning of the Lost Cause. He shunned many of the qualities that colored the writing of Confederate rationalists *within* the South. His writing ignored the tedious political rationalizations that dominated the work of Jefferson Davis and Alexander Stephens. Cooke also shunned the theological soul searching that haunted even the pages of veterans' magazines such as the *Southern Historical Society Papers*. He wrote no pitiable diatribes on how southerners were better people because northern soldiers were cowards and bullies who possessed only superior manpower. He eschewed the defensive tone that colored the writing of such contemporaries as the Reverend John William Jones or Jubal Early and Daniel Harvey Hill. Cooke realized that carping and self-pity were unnecessary; a writer could ensnare the foe with the honey instead of the vinegar.

The enemy was immune to the bitter complaints of former Rebels, but he was extremely vulnerable to talented local color writers of the new romanticism in the postwar years. Cooke was a superb romantic writer who used his talents in part as a means to justify the Confederate tradition. He did this by concentrating upon positive factors. Themes seldom varied from three fundamental concepts—the genteel, patriotic heritage of colonial Virginia; the noble, pleasing qualities of antebellum planter life in the Old Dominion; and the superior qualities of human character produced by two such backgrounds.

Some northern responses to Cooke's writings reveal his significance to the Lost Cause rationale. After his 1883 state history of Virginia was published, a reviewer in the New York *Sun* observed that "it would not be easy to speak of this performance in terms of too hearty commendation," because, next to New England, "Virginia has exercised the most decisive . . . influence upon the character and fortunes of the composite American people." Meanwhile a writer in the New York *Times* insisted that Virginia was "the only part of the country that went into the war or came out of it with any credit," while the Springfield *Republican* described Cooke's romantic portrayal of Virginia life as "an accurate depiction."

More prophetic of the future national mood was an 1882

sketch of Cooke in the Philadelphia *American's* Living American Authors series. The author viewed Cooke as representative of a peculiar nobility possessed by Virginia:

> When John Randolph said "When I speak of my country, I mean the State of Virginia!" he uttered a sentiment which more or less influenced every man, woman and child in the proud Commonwealth. It was this feeling which made Robert E. Lee resist all the brilliant prospects held out to him by General Scott, and cast his fortunes with Virginia. It was this same feeling which made John Esten Cooke throw down his pen, and abandon the literary pursuits which he loved so well, and take up the sword in the cause of Virginia.

John Esten Cooke did not live to see the real meaning of these statements take effect in northern attitudes toward the old Confederacy. He died of typhoid fever in 1886, while working on another romantic novel planned for serialization in a Detroit newspaper. It is fitting that Cooke's uncle, the Federal general Philip St. George Cooke, whose daughter had married John Esten Cooke's comrade J. E. B. Stuart, presented a stained-glass window to the family church in memory of his nephew.

John Esten Cooke's wartime and postwar writing career produced some twenty-three books and enough articles—mostly in northern periodicals—to fill an additional dozen or more volumes. Even if he had not been regarded as the premier southern writer in the waning years of Reconstruction, the sheer amount of his literary output would demand attention.

Cooke's role in the Confederate apology was that of a transitional figure. Unfortunately, often he has been viewed as being merely a highly successful southern local color writer of the late nineteenth century.

Actually Cooke's great contribution to the Lost Cause generation is extremely difficult to categorize. He was a bridge between those two bodies of Lost Cause writers who wrote for two distinct audiences—the defeated South and the national reading public. In part he shared characteristics of both, but he belongs in neither group.

The bitter quality of the immediate postwar Confederate writers lingered even into the early twentieth century. These men, such as Jubal Early and Parson John William Jones, possessed a self-destructive nature, a Hamlet-like sense of tragedy that pervaded their writings in the Reconstruction era. Even a cursory examination of their avenues of public outcry, such as *Southern Magazine, Southern Review,* or *Southern Historical Society Papers,* cannot obscure their psychological trauma, theological self-searching, and bullish conviction that honor and purity were the province of the South.

The deep anger never disappeared entirely. On the eve of the First World War, the pages of the *Confederate Veteran* magazine bore a strong resemblance to the Lost Cause periodicals of Reconstruction days. Even the players often were the same— the indomitable Early, Jones, Gordon, and others.

Still, the passage of time softened the vituperation. Even former Rebels were not immune to the romantic theme, and by the eighties the defenders of the Inner Lost Cause were viewing the war as a great, heroic epic. It was a nostalgic looking backward by men who had been caught up in what was the Great Experience of their lives. Events had drawn them from drab experiences in Opelika, Alabama, or Gaffney, South Carolina, to march in huge armies that for a time had brought terror to citizens of Philadelphia or Cincinnati.

When they returned from Appomattox, stark contrast between their humdrum daily lives and the glories of serving under "Marse" Robert were exaggerated by their abysmal poverty. Steadily, for these people, the war became a great saga. A survivor of General Jeb Stuart's cavalry could recall that "the memory of those days seems like a beautiful dream—seen even through the mists of rolling years."

Their nostalgia was the most extreme form of southern romanticism in the late nineteenth century. It contained a far more extreme variety than did the descriptions of southern life provided by those who wrote to justify the Confederacy to the rest of the world. By the 1880s, the advocates of the Inner Lost Cause fixed upon the theme that the Rebel effort in the Civil War had been a grand and gallant epic by men of knightly qualities. Always, General Robert E. Lee was held up as the epitome of such a courtly society. One Louisville writer asserted that Lee's ancestry dated to Robert the Bruce of Scotland, and another maintained that Lee could be traced to "Launcelot Lee . . . who accompanied William the Conqueror."

The overemphasis on chivalry by southern rationalists provided solace to a generation of veterans, but it did not win the real Lost Cause. The years of orations at veterans' reunions, speeches at the dedication of Confederate monuments, and articles in the *Southern Bivouac* or *Confederate Veteran* contained a romantic quality characterized by two features. There was an excessive quality to the self-praise for chivalry that, to the northern reader, would appear at best unreal, if not downright absurd. Typical was a toast by one Major C. S. Stringfellow at an 1886 Richmond reunion of veterans of Pegram's battalion. The good major recalled the unit's exploits as providing "an example of heroic daring and unflinching courage which finds no parallel. . . . What bright leaves all in the chaplet which the valor of the Confederate infantry wove into its immortal crown!" Meanwhile at another gathering of veterans, a speaker described the righteous quality of Confederate soldiers: "I do affirm that, perhaps, never in the world's history were gathered together such large bodies of men who were so generally pervaded by a deep and strong religious spirit. . . . Lee is the noblest type of a Christian warrior that our century has produced; nay, stands peerless among the sons of men of every nationality and of every age." Such statements evoked the scorn of outsiders. An editor of the Minneapolis *Tribune*, as late as 1890, sneered at southern attempts to cloak Lee "with a sort of halo of moral grandeur, military genius and knightly grace."

John Esten Cooke's romantic descriptions of the Confederacy avoided both the argumentative tone and the excess of emotion displayed by the Confederate justifiers. Certainly his writings were fanciful enough. His *Mohun: Or the Last Days of Lee and His Paladins* contained such ingredients as a Confederate general suffering from loss of memory, a black sorceress, an attempted poisoning, and a bevy of sinister espionage agents.

Generally, however, his approach was more wistful than boasting, and involved looking back to the halcyon days of the Old Dominion rather than indulging in the bitterness of contemporary problems. Cooke's memory stopped with Appomattox. Thereafter, his writings were not offered as a defense, but as a description of a gentle, chivalric pastoral society that he believed had existed and was now gone forever. Even rival Virginia authors could be touched by Cooke's descriptions of the old life. George Cary Eggleston, after receiving a letter from Cooke, commented that "it carried me back, in fancy, to the dear old days which have drifted so far away that I can hardly think of them except as a memory of some former state of existence—a beautiful vision—a dream from which we have been rudely awakened."

John Esten Cooke was never "rudely awakened" from that memory. Until his death his writing remained one-dimensional—to delight his readers with descriptions of Virginia's culture. This was the end in itself for the author. Cooke was a professional writer, not a crusader. He wrote less to justify the South than to

intrigue the Yankee reader with accounts of Virginia life. His reading audience was the burgeoning middle-class America of the
waning years of Reconstruction. His readers wanted to be enter-
tained by tales of the South's charm, not proselytized by the Confederate myth.

The missionary effort that produced a national conversion to
many Lost Cause ideals had begun by the time of John Esten
Cooke's death. Cooke's vital contribution to the process of southern justification was in serving as a transitional figure. In the seventies and early eighties, he led the phalanx of southern authors—
mainly Virginians—who gained a national audience in northern
magazines and newspapers.

Cooke, by far the most well known of this vanguard, was a
bridge between the Inner Lost Cause and the real Lost Cause rationale. Certainly he did not share that die-hard Confederate mentality of Jubal Early, Alexander Stephens, and Alfred Bledsoe. For
fifty years this ever-dwindling generation refought the war and
sectional issues in reunion speeches and veterans' magazines.

Meanwhile, by the late 1880s, a talented, influential body of
southern writers—mainly Virginians—were attempting a different approach. Thomas Nelson Page, Sara Pryor, and many others
shunned the old neo-Confederate isolationism; instead, they
fought the real Lost Cause on northern soil. They breached the
parapets of Yankee resistance in national magazines by portraying
a far different image of the South.

The core of the new image was the presentation of Virginia as
the epitome of the finest elements found in the South. Already by
the early eighties, because of the influence of Cooke and other
early local colorists, the nation's attention had been drawn to Virginia as a place of special charm. Yet Cooke's style could not gain
acceptance for the Lost Cause. His writings were, in the main, escapist romanticism. In a nation increasingly attuned to the pragmatic faith, his brand of nostalgia possessed absolute, defined lim-
its. And although his pastoral Virginia delighted readers, it was

only a portrait of Virginia *as was*, in the author's eyes. What did it portend for the present and future?

The new Lost Cause school used the touchstone of Virginia's unique role in the southern experience and fashioned a powerful image that gained considerable national acceptance by the First World War. One observes in the late Reconstruction years the slow development of a persuasive approach that has yet to fail in receiving a favorable response from outsiders. Gone was Cooke's one-sided picture of idyllic Virginia. The new national image was that of a dualistic South, at once romantic and tragic. It was a convincing appeal that evoked both admiration and sympathy. One could almost choose which South he preferred. On one hand there was the Romantic South; on the other the Tragic South. The image of the Romantic South provided by the new generation of writers was far more sophisticated than the older Cooke nostalgia. It offered more than a montage of jasmine, contented servants, and palatial homes. There was still enough of this, as in Sara Pryor's haunting *My Day: Reminiscences of a Long Life*, where she described childhood experiences in elegant Virginia gardens "everywhere; abloom with roses, lilies, violets, jonquils, flowering almond trees which never fruited, double-flowering peach trees. . . . No cavalier of that day would present to his ladye faire the simple flowers we love today."

Perhaps more representative of the new romanticism was Thomas Nelson Page's observation on Virginia's culture in his *Stories of the Old Dominion*: "It was by no mere accident that George Washington, Patrick Henry, Thomas Jefferson, George Mason, Edmund Pendleton . . . came from the shores of the rivers which poured into the Chesapeake. They were the product of the life established on those shores."

The "product of the life" was the core of the Romantic South. The trappings of John Esten Cooke's land of charm now bore an importance beyond themselves. They were only part of a cultural mosaic that was at once a finer life that produced better people. Thus Thomas Nelson Page would suggest that his Virginians still rested their lives on "the old fountains . . . the old standards of gentility and righteousness of life."

But had this been all there was to the new rationale, it would have proven insufficient to alter national opinion. Certainly there would be the question of how a finer society could keep three and one-half million people in bondage. One senses, however, that this would not have been the prime objection to a bilateral romantic image. Racism was a national problem in the era of reunion. Even surface ripples of the problem make this fact undeniable—the 1896 and 1898 Supreme Court decisions, the influence of the Dunning School in American historical studies, the national response to Thomas Dixon's 1905 *The Clansman*, and many others.

The northern public media in the waning Reconstruction years said relatively little about the slavery issue, but often spoke of disloyalty. If the society made better men, how could they commit treason by fighting against the old flag? If Robert E. Lee were representative of the flower of Virginia civilization, how could he abandon three decades of service to the army, reject a Union command, and support the rebellion? After all, as a speaker observed in 1890 before a gathering of Union veterans, "thus did Colonel Lee forsake the grandest government of earth, dishonor the fairest flag of nations," and consequently imprint "treason on the foreheads of his posterity."

More in keeping with the national mood of that same year, however, was a comment in *Harper's Weekly*. The author described the dedication of the Lee monument in Richmond and observed that "General Lee personified what was best in a bad cause. His individual virtues gave the Southern people . . . something substantial and unquestionably creditable to rally around."

Perhaps the writer in *Harper's* was a convert to the other face of the Lost Cause argument, that of the Tragic South. The same late-nineteenth-century southern authors who described the superior ideals and culture of the Romantic South also used the reverse side of the blade. Ironically, the other cutting edge of the Lost Cause reasoning employed the tactics of hated foes, Social Darwinism and pragmatism.

The Tragic South imagery was based upon the Darwinian idea that man was a product of his environment. Immediately after the war Confederate authors flailed angrily at the concept that the best institutions survive. Certainly Darwin's ideas were still quite new in 1865, but the Calvinistic ideal that merit and success are intertwined was an old American axiom. When Herbert Spencer's Social Darwinism gained a following in the post-Reconstruction years, it would appear that the Yankee argument had received massive reinforcement. If the fittest institutions survive, then why did the Confederacy perish?

But another generation of southern authors and lecturers met this new northern challenge in the last decades of the nineteenth century. These spokesmen for the Confederacy chose to borrow the enemy's tactics instead of attacking him headlong. The enemy was Social Darwinism and its concept of the survival of the strongest institutions, which reinforced the older Calvinist and puritan ethic of the success-grace relationship.

Here is the supreme irony of the entire Lost Cause argument. The Confederate mentality evident in immediate postwar writings and later publications such as the *Confederate Veteran* flailed angrily—and hopelessly—at the buoyant Yankee insistence that the war's outcome was sheer physical evidence that the southern cause was unfit for a role in a new America. Now the South's advocates seized upon the same reasoning, modified the tactics slightly, and wielded a rationalization that proved difficult to refute.

If any single quality describes the South's literary output from the 1880s until the First World War, it is the heavy emphasis upon environmentalism. This is the core of the Tragic South reasoning, and it was used to explain the thorns of both secession and defeat. Shaped cautiously by a generation of novelists, orators, and historians, it was indeed almost impossible to refute.

Secession was a product of environment. Soil, climate, and other features produced a unique culture possessed of grace, honor, and chivalric manners. These romantic elements were offset by the presence of slavery and a militant southern isolationism that contributed eventually to secession.

Sometimes even the intractable Confederate veteran utilized this environment apology for secession. An example was the professor-soldier General Daniel Harvey Hill, whose hatred of Yankees certainly predated Fort Sumter. In 1887 Hill delivered a veterans' reunion speech in Baltimore on the topic "The Old South." Certainly no one would expect Hill, a former corps leader in the Confederate army, to disavow completely the old die-hard mode of thinking. So there were ample references to the Grant scandals, which occurred "when the Old South was out of power." Of these misdeeds, "frauds known as the Emma Mine stock, Seneca Stone contract, Whiskey Ring Swindles, Pacific Mail subsidies, sales of Sutlers' Posts, steals of Government lands, back salary grabs," to Hill the point was obvious. "When Southern statesmen had a controlling influence, these knaveries were unknown," because no official from "the Old South . . . was ever charged with roguery."

Thus far Hill's address was a stereotype of the better-man concept of the era of apologists such as Alexander Stephens and Jubal Early. But then he probed the question of why was the South different, and what produced secession? For Hill, slavery, southern isolationism, and secession were environmental factors. Hence, "The Northern States of the Old Thirteen had magnificent bays and harbors, but a bleak, inhospitable climate, in which African slaves could not thrive." Meanwhile, the South "had a quality of soil and climate well suited to the African." As a result, "the people of the Old South maintained slavery and devoted themselves almost exclusively to agriculture." Thus, "cut off from wealth" in manufacturing, commerce, and other pursuits, southerners found only two fields open in which they achieved distinction, and became "leading statesmen and reknowned warriors."

When the war came and was lost, again it was a result of forces beyond the control of brave, superior men. Absent from Hill's analysis was the older fixation upon what Bernard De-Voto labeled in the 1930s as the "Everlasting If" that slept "uneasily" in southern blood. The war was not lost by some chance rifled-musket shots in the gloomy thicket at Chancellorsville where "Stonewall" Jackson perished, or in some crucial hours on July 2 in General James Longstreet's field headquarters at Gettysburg.

Later, the sage journalist Henry Watterson would assert that an agrarian southland was "doomed in its cradle" when it contested the rising industrial might of the North. Even stubborn Harvey Hill would suggest this. For Hill, the southern defeat was a tragic example of environmental influence: "We had been dependent upon the North for everything, even for the paper upon which the Ordinances of Secession were written, and for the ink and pens used in the writing. . . . We rushed into war, not only without ships of war and trade, but without a single mill to make powder in the whole Confederacy. . . . We were without mines, without factories, foundries, machine shops, roller mills—without mechanical appliances of every kind."

The multifaced Lost Cause reasoning was an awesome weapon. The Romantic and Tragic South images did not appear inconsistent. Many authors used both themes simultaneously, and Dixie benefited from having the proverbial best of both worlds.

After all, what was contradictory in descriptions of a Romantic South of better people, such as Robert E. Lee, who were driven in tragic fashion by external forces to support slavery and secession?

The dual image was even more appealing, because from a national viewpoint the core of the Lost Cause image was Virginia—not the entire South. From the 1880s until the First World War, a large body of southern novelists, essayists, orators, and historians by concentrating upon Virginia actually strove to justify the South. Virginia became the showplace of all that was romantic and tragic in the Confederate experience.

There are several intriguing matters concerning this Lost Cause rationale, an argument far different from that offered by the generation of Jefferson Davis. In fact, the argument sometimes involved a disparagement of Virginia's southern neighbors. George Cary Eggleston, for example, bore hard upon the absolute dichotomy of Virginia's regard for the Union in 1861 and that of the cotton South's leaders. To Eggleston, the Deep South advocates of secession were "types of a class which brought upon the South a deal of odium," and were people characterized by "their bragging, their intolerance, their contempt for the North, their arrogance." Such men forced Virginia into the war. Although they disapproved of slavery and secession, Virginians believed that the Federal government could not coerce an errant state. When President Abraham Lincoln issued a call for troops to suppress the rebellion, Virginians had to choose between dishonor and the grievous task of leaving the Union. To Eggleston, "they could not, without cowardice and dishonor, do otherwise, and Virginians are brave men and honorable ones."

Here is another supreme irony in the Lost Cause argument. The Virginia writers, such as Eggleston, Thomas Nelson Page, and Constance Cary Harrison, bore hard upon the dissimilarities between the Old Dominion and the cotton South. Even a casual observer, however, might question this line of reasoning. If Virginia had remained such a hallmark of Jeffersonian liberalism in a slavocracy dominated by the thinking of John C. Calhoun, then why did it take such an active part in the war? More precisely, if General Robert E. Lee's resignation from the United States Army involved a degree of remorse that seemed unparalleled, then why did he turn instantly and plunge immediately into the Rebel war effort?

These two images appeared to create a dilemma for Virginia writers. On one hand, they sought to emphasize their role in creating the nation, and to stress the intense love Virginians held for the Union. Also, however, Virginians desired to be identified as the leaders of the Confederate war effort. How could the Old Dominion boast of the heritage of a Jefferson and a "Jeb" Stuart simultaneously?

The solution was not very difficult. At once Virginia became the central part of that double image of romance and tragedy. The romantic element was the description of a life style that had produced a superior race of men. In turn, this civilization had become entrapped in an environmental web of slavery and secession, reacted in 1861 out of an ingrained sense of honor, and suffered tragic consequences. Clearly, romance, tragedy, and Virginia were the dominant topics of the rising National Lost Cause.

Such was the case with George Cary Eggleston, a Hoosier schoolteacher with strong family ties in the Old Dominion. His long career of writing on his beloved Virginia, "the greatest joy I have known in life," included important novels such as *The Warrens of Virginia* and *The Master of Warlock*, a massive *History of the Confederate States*, and charming reminiscences such as *A Rebel's Recollections* and *Recollections of a Varied Life*. Eggleston's literary career spanned four decades of, as he described it, writing "of the old Virginia life as I remember it." He never deviated from a course described in an 1874 letter to his friend John Esten Cooke, that he wrote in the hope that his work would "change some people's views of the South and Southerners."

That same year he issued in serialized form "A Rebel's Recollections" in *Atlantic Monthly*, which was received so well in the North that it was issued soon after in hardcover. In this pioneer series of articles, Eggleston established a basic pattern used later by many other authors and lecturers.

The formula was a tale of romance and tragedy based upon the saga of Virginia. Because of their breeding, Virginians possessed a special grace, sense of humor, and love for the Union. Eggleston did not go as far as some later southern Lost Cause writers who insisted Virginians did not believe in slavery. But he emphasized—as did later writers—the difference between citizens of the commonwealth and those of the South at large. Virginians "heartily condemned the secession of South Carolina and the rest" and felt "a good deal of indignation" against the hotheads.

From the 1880s until the First World War, the Eggleston pattern was repeated by scores of southern historians, novelists, and essayists. The new Lost Cause, fashioned for a national reading public, was more Virginia than the South. It keyed upon the dualism of Virginia's romance and tragedy, and stressed the fortunes of Robert E. Lee as the archetypal example.

Such themes dominated the fiction of Thomas Nelson Page in "Marse Chan" and *Red Rock* and Eggleston in *The Warrens of Virginia*. It was the core of important war reminiscences, such as Constance Cary Harrison's *Recollections Grave and Gay*, Sara Pryor's *Reminiscences of Peace and War*, Robert E. Lee, Jr.'s *Recollections and Letters of General Robert E. Lee*, Robert Stiles's *Four Years with Marse Robert*, Myrta Avery's *A Virginia Girl in the Civil War*, and many other influential works. Historians and biographers such as Philip Alexander Bruce, Henry White, and Fitzhugh Lee plied the same themes.

The national reaction after 1900 to the new southern image has been well documented. Still, one never ceases to marvel at the onrush of enthusiasm for the new Lost Cause evident among northern reviewers. The New York *Daily Mirror* praised Constance Cary Harrison's *Recollections* as a "valuable and moving" account of "noble men," while the Albany, New York, *Press* praised her "valuable and fascinating writing." The Philadelphia *Public Ledger* described Sara Pryor's reminiscences as "essential to the true understanding of history," and necessary reading for Americans "who would see the full conditions of the South in its great crisis." The New York *Times* noted that Robert E. Lee, Jr., brought out his father's "modesty, the courage, the humility and the grandeur of soul" in such a manner "that scorners were subdued to contrition." Meanwhile, a reviewer in *Current Literature* spoke of the "remarkable reception in every section" accorded to Captain Lee's book.

The marked change in national attitudes toward the Confederacy by the first decade of the twentieth century is well documented in Paul Buck's *Road to Reunion* and many other sources. Certainly the factors that prompted a softening of sectional resentment were at once complex and varied. Like the wind, they are understood better by observing evidences of their presence. Here one encounters a myriad of meaningful images of reunion—the popularity of Generals Fitzhugh Lee and Joseph Wheeler in the Spanish-American War; Robert E. Lee's 1901 induction into the Hall of Fame; General Joe Johnston's presence at the funeral of his old adversary William Sherman; Charles Francis Adams' famous address at Washington and Lee University during the 1907 Lee birthday commemoration; and the poignant gathering of the blue and gray at the 1913 long encampment of Gettysburg.

The popularity of the new southern image did much to clear the path toward a new surge of national reunion after 1900. Actually the writers of the National Lost Cause did far more than

Chapter Three

ROBERT E. LEE AND THE SOUTHERN MIND

We know so much about him, or at least we believe we do. By the measure of most prominent men, there should be nothing left to tell of the private life and military feats of Robert E. Lee.

What else can be told of one so awesome that his shadow falls across the entire southern presence in American life? We know of his early, dutiful attendance to an ailing mother, a model record at the military academy, and a pattern of abstemious habits molded early in life. Anyone who has read of Robert E. Lee can recite other parts of that canon of devotion to the supreme southern hero symbol.

There was his marriage to Mary Custis, the "child of Arlington," and the subsequent decades of devotion to a sickly wife." One reads of Lee's skill and courage in the difficult campaign from Vera Cruz to Mexico City, when his daring and judgment forever earned him the admiration of General Winfield Scott.

The Mexican War and its newspaper accolades passed, and eventually many destined for later greatness in the Civil War grew weary of slow promotion, low pay, and dusty outpost duty. Ulysses Grant, William Sherman, George Meade, P. G. T. Beauregard—all ventured into civilian life. We know that Lee remained for well over a decade in a tedious, often lonely existence that tested his resolve early. His letters during these years are in the public domain and have been printed in scores of books. He languished over absence from his ailing wife and his beloved Virginia soil. Lee fretted about his inability to supervise more closely the daily temptations that beset a gathering brood of seven children. So he often wrote letters to his offspring, urging them to adopt a code of Christian service and duty, to mind their manners and recite prayers. The once private messages from a father to his children are now a matter of public record.

We know that Robert E. Lee himself uttered prayers daily and demonstrated other mannerisms of a Christian gentleman. Grammar school children in Alabama a half-century ago could recite those Lee traits that still evoke admiration even from the pens of skeptics. For a New South generation, Lee epitomized duty, humility, self-denial, and practice of self-control.

Duty became that habit most often associated with the Virginian. Presidents from Theodore Roosevelt to Jimmy Carter have invoked the Lee legend in political addresses. The devotion of Robert E. Lee to the maxim of duty has caught the attention of schoolchildren, scholars, popular magazine journalists, and advertising specialists. Forgotten is Lee's choice to fight against the old flag in 1861.

Much is known of the events that followed that most fateful decision of Lee's career in 1861. The well-known saga of his wartime exploits made it appear that fate moved Lee to greatness. First came the slow rise to prominence amid some public disapproval in the first year of the war. Then there was the chance shot at Seven Pines that disabled General Joseph Johnston and allowed Lee to display brilliance against the Army of the Potomac in the Seven Days'. Within months Lee's name engendered fear and admiration in northern camps, as he wrecked the reputations of several Union commanders.

The surrender at Appomattox Courthouse did not bring this admiration to an end. Certainly during the sectional bitterness of the Reconstruction era, Lee's name, like those of most former Rebels, was persona non grata in the Yankee press. Yet the lofty character and goodness of Lee were discussed time and again by national magazines by the end of the nineteenth century. After 1900 came a torrent of articles on Lee the man, not the soldier. Authors described the pet hen kept at his headquarters, how he rescued a fledgling sparrow while under enemy artillery fire, prayers said daily at the headquarters of the Army of Northern Virginia, and countless other vignettes. In 1901 Lee became one of the first inductees into the new Hall of Fame, the *Ladies' Home Journal* delighted readers with tales of his love for animals, and Teddy Roosevelt called Lee a "matter of pride to all our countrymen."

One could argue that all of this never should have happened. How could Americans forget that Lee was the vaunted Rebel chieftain whose army had destroyed thousands of northern men and boys? More important, he was the *defeated* Rebel. Lee had failed, and he bore the image of loser in an American society becoming more steeped in success as merit. This pragmatic bent, the belief that the *outcome* is the justification, characterized the American mind long before William James and John Burgess. Those earlier European observers of our new national landscape, such as Alexis de Tocqueville, had noticed our obsession with the successful and the practical.

The resolution of this enigma was provided in 1908 by an observer in the New York *Times*. Robert E. Lee, Jr., had published in 1904 the highly influential *Recollections and Letters of Robert E. Lee*, and national response to the book was overwhelmingly favorable. The younger Lee, blending his own reminiscences with the General's personal letters, fashioned a new image of his father, not a military figure, but a man possessed of admirable traits—gentleness, humility, a love of duty, and even a love for his nation. The New York *Times* commented that, until this book was published, "his true character was not fully understood . . . the modesty, the courage, the humility and the grandeur of soul."

Much of the grandeur was in Lee's acceptance of defeat in 1865, and we know much about this as well. This story of his postwar career has been told so often that we can conjure up these images easily—the wise leader who counseled acceptance of defeat; the unselfish Lee who refused to sell his reputation to insurance companies for gain and chose a presidency at humble Washington College; the New South advocate who spurned talking of the war and worked to prepare a generation of young men for an uncertain future; and the magnanimous Lee, who refused to stoop to the carping and petty debates of war issues that marred the conduct of other former Confederate generals.

All of these elements of the Lee image were found in southern literature by the end of the Reconstruction era. Since then, the basic tenets of the Lee story have emerged again and again in increasing numbers of books, articles, and other printed matter. A virtual torrent of commentary on Lee appeared after 1900, when the General finally achieved a total national acceptance as a hero figure; the southern renascence of the nineteen-twenties and thirties brought a new rush of interest in Robert E. Lee and the Civil War. The shelves of libraries groaned again in the 1950s as the nation faced the war's centennial observance. The immense literature of the Civil War centennial possessed two undeniable characteristics. Much of the writing was tawdry, hastily prepared, and cynically commercial. More important, the life and military exploits of Lee ranked along with the leadership of Lincoln as a dominant subject.

By the end of the Civil War centennial, the national reading public was weary of the whole affair. Almost every possible topic had been mined by the literary market. Bookstalls overflowed with third-rate biographies of fourth-rate generals; the *Saturday Evening Post* even featured an article on a rag doll that had belonged to the McLean family and had been in the room where Lee and Grant met to sign the surrender. The brilliant southern literary critic, Louis Rubin, Jr., attempted to plead for some literary standards in a tongue-in-cheek article titled "Lee's Surgeon's Horse." Even Rubin threw up his hands in despair, noting that "the fact is that Civil War scholarship *pays*. It pays very well. 'Lee's Surgeon's Horse' has joined 'Lincoln's Doctor's Dog' as a recipe for bestsellers."

Even before this onslaught of writing, the bibliography of Lee's career was immense. Douglas Southall Freeman's classic *R. E. Lee* provided a huge listing of printed materials existing in the 1930s. Almost two months later, in 1951, William Hollis and Marshall Fishwick issued another compilation, *A Preliminary Checklist of Writings About R. E. Lee.*

Obviously these experts were aware that their compilations listed only those basic printed materials. Dr. Freeman's comment that his list was designed to be "critical rather than comprehensive" was a self-acknowledged understatement. With the exception of George Washington, no other American has been the subject of more books and articles.

A complete bibliography of writings on Robert E. Lee would fill several volumes on a library shelf. The number of separate printed items certainly runs into the tens of thousands and probably more. The biographies, studies of military campaigns, and reminiscences of those who knew Lee are only the tip of the iceberg. There are thousands of newspaper articles, from the Fort Sumter era until the present, in addition to printed funeral orations; articles in veterans' magazines such as *Southern Bivouac* and *Confederate Veteran*; printed speeches delivered at dusty reunion camps; romantic poetry and fiction; the massive writings on Gettysburg; the advertisements of Confederate memorial associations; the public relations literature of Washington and Lee University; popular magazine vignettes, from the aged *Lippincott's* to the modern *Reader's Digest*, and many other writings.

Here rests one of the great ironies of the Civil War. The immense amount of writing about Robert E. Lee reflects a belief of devotion by southerners that he was the central figure of the Confederate experience. This devotion dates back to the ashes of defeat. When the South of Reconstruction years passed, Lee already had become almost immortal in the southern mind. He was transformed from a great military leader into an invincible chieftain, from a man of superb character into one without flaw.

Long before 1900, Lee had become the quintessential proof of the Lost Cause creed that good men sometimes lose, that the righteous do not prevail always. The legends surrounding him would grow in time; already by 1907, the centennial year of his birth, the intensity of southern veneration for Lee possessed almost religious overtones. As biographer Marshall Fishwick observed, Lee became the closest being to a saint possessed by a white Protestant South.

The irony is that while the South selected Lee as the hallmark of both the war and its culture, those who loved him most knew him least. He has never been understood by his own people. One must return again to that perceptive query by the canny wartime observer, Mary Boykin Chesnut, who asked, "Can anyone say that they know Robert E. Lee?"

The southern mind has never felt easy in the presence of Robert E. Lee. Even during the war years themselves, when most in the public eye, he remained an abstract being, possessed of a quality of greatness no one could equal but nevertheless should aspire to emulate. He has been always the *ideal*, not the reality, for wholesome southern youth to imitate.

A spirit of reverence has always marked the southerner's approach to Robert E. Lee, a setting apart of the General. One observes it even during the war, years before the image of Lee developed a superhuman aura. There was, for example, that poignant reunion in 1864 of Lee and the men of General James Longstreet's corps, who had been absent for almost eight months on the western front. When Lee appeared at the corps review, there was a spontaneous cheer that lapsed quickly into a reverential silence. General Porter Alexander described the effect as "of a military sacrament." A South Carolina soldier recalled that as Lee passed, men broke ranks to touch his leg, his horse, or even the animal's bridle, noting that "anything that Lee had was sacred."

In the years after General Lee's death, as his hero status increased to near sainthood, his memory became a nonpersonal abstraction for the Confederate generation. Lee became unlike a southerner at all, with the predictable exaggerations of temper, politics, or even moral behavior. Rather, he steadily became an ideal. There was a coldness in this image that did not mesh with the temperament of a Mississippi dirt farmer or a Charleston politician.

The abstraction was there immediately after Lee's death in late 1870. The following day, a bevy of Rebel veterans and local civilians gathered in the small Rockbridge County Courthouse at Lexington to pass a resolution honoring his memory. Amid the grief, the assembly voted thanks to God "that to us was the honor and the blessing of communion with him in his last days on earth." Meanwhile, across the little valley at Washington College, Professor William Preston Johnston addressed the faculty and students, describing Lee as "without one blemish, one spot, one stain."

Always, Robert E. Lee has remained set apart from a people who selected him as their absolute hero figure. In the age of the Confederate veteran, Lee was to Georgia's Senator Ben Hill, the "private citizen without wrong . . . a man without guile." A former Rebel eulogized Lee at a Petersburg veterans' meeting as "purest, truest, greatest—there was none like him, none!" Meanwhile another speaker at a Richmond reunion meeting described him as "so blameless as might become a saint." In the southern renascence of the 1930s, James Young, in his

Marse Robert: Knight of the Confederacy, even suggested that "it may be doubted whether Lee ever committed an act that would reflect upon his moral self," while his eminent biographer, Douglas Freeman, styled the General as "one of the greatest human beings of modern time." Later, in the centennial years, one Dixie speaker described Lee as a "vanquished victor of the stainless soul," destined for "an undisputed place in the halls of universal fame."

All of this has an important meaning far beyond the rhetoric and the devotion that inspired it. One clue to divining the relationship between Lee and the southern mode of thinking came in a 1909 speech by Woodrow Wilson at the University of North Carolina. Wilson, then head of Princeton University, delivered the annual Lee birthday address before a large audience of state legislators and members of the university community. In his introduction, Wilson admitted that no words of praise could elevate Lee to a higher plane, because the General was "in some regards unapproachable in the history of our country."

The essential word is *unapproachable.* To a Dixie society that cherishes close personal relationships, Lee has remained apart, a counterweight to the southerner's own sense of mortality.

For example, it is difficult to imagine a meeting between Robert E. Lee and one of our contemporary southern hero-folk individuals such as "Bear" Bryant, stock-car racer Richard Petty, or singer Waylon Jennings. It is easier to envision these modern Dixie celebrities with some other Civil War heroes, such as General Joseph Johnston, whose troops loved to pat his bald head affectionately, or with other legendary Rebels such as "Stonewall" Jackson or "Jeb" Stuart. Lee's reverential image would intimidate even a "Bear" Bryant, and one conjectures that the meeting would be an uneasy one.

Southerners have never understood Robert E. Lee and have

been intimidated by his godlike image. Always, there has been a gulf between the steadiness and purity of Lee's image and the paradoxes and extremes that characterize the southern mind.

Still, there is more to Woodrow Wilson's "unapproachable" Lee than the power of his hero mystique. The other great hero of the Civil War, Abraham Lincoln, is revered as much by the nation at large as is Lee by his southern brethren. Lincoln's image, too, has developed almost superhuman traits—sage, philosopher, liberator, humanitarian, military genius. But to a Kansas schoolchild, Lincoln is also a person, the rough-hewn gangling youth, the awkward and crude prairie lawyer.

The solution to the enigmatic love and detachment southerners feel for Lee rests in some factors beyond the sheer power of his hero status. In part, the answer can be found in the southerner's conception of why Robert E. Lee is the supreme hero. Two years before Woodrow Wilson's North Carolina address, the nation observed the centennial of Lee's birthday. The cultural implications of this event may have been underrated by scholars. In the South it was a massive display of affection involving school programs, religious services, banquets, and political oratory.

The size and extent of Lee birthday observances indicated his position as a veritable southern saint. All other hero symbols of the Confederacy had faded into secondary positions. During the war, "Stonewall" Jackson competed with Lee for the southern heart, but by 1907 he was remembered more as Lee's eccentric, brilliant subordinate. P. G. T. Beauregard, Joseph Johnston, and others had suffered a similar fate, although their presence or mention of their names could still evoke poignant outbursts of emotion at a veterans' reunion.

But none could match the hero status of Robert E. Lee. Lee was no longer the great war figure but was the great southerner, exemplifying the finest virtues of a good life destroyed by the

Industrial Revolution. This canonization of Lee was a common theme in southern writings during the celebration of his birthday centennial.

It takes nothing away from devotion to Lee's memory to suggest that more was involved here than mere devotion to the General. The writings suggest as well a feeling of *vindication*, of conviction that through the new popular image of Lee in the nation, the entire Rebel cause had, at last, been justified. Lee was the gentle agrarian, the representative of a finer life that the South had fought to preserve, rather than the onerous institution of slavery.

Such vindication was not without opposition. As late as 1890 a Philadelphia newspaper compared the General to Benedict Arnold, asserting that "Robert E. Lee betrayed his trust." An Indianapolis editor referred to the new equestrian statue of Lee in Richmond as "sculptured treason," and a writer in the Minneapolis *Tribune* charged that Lee "lacked the stuff that the highest type of hero is made of."

Within almost a decade, general national opinion of Lee had reversed sharply, so much so that it surprised northerners themselves. Occasionally a Yankee editor wrote in amazement at the new outpouring of national affection for Lee, evident after his 1901 induction into the Hall of Fame. Typical was the response of the popular *Outlook* magazine. In 1906 an entire issue was devoted to Lee's career. The editor praised Lee's "stainless life," and said that "the nation has a hero to place beside her greatest." Still, the editor admitted that if anyone four decades previous had suggested that such national adulation for Lee would develop, "he would have been regarded as an unpatriotic lunatic." Meanwhile, a writer in *Harper's Weekly* observed that "probably no one would have ventured . . . that the American people at the beginning of the twentieth century, would be claiming Robert E. Lee . . . as the pride of the whole country."

But the nation did claim Lee, and elevated him to a hero status shared only by a handful of individuals, such as Washington, Lincoln, and Jefferson. A writer in *Harper's* proclaimed him "the pride of the whole country," another journalist in the *Chautauquan* insisted that he was "in the first triumvirate of greatness" with Lincoln and Washington. The New York *Times* praised Lee's "grandeur of soul," and *Nation* called Lee "great in gentleness and goodness."

Much of the southern writing on Lee in his centennial years displayed a self-conscious awareness of the General's new status. In his 1906 biography, *Life of Robert E. Lee,* Henry Shepherd exulted that Lee was now "the whole world's darling," while Robert Stiles's popular reminiscence, *Four Years with Marse Robert* boasted that Lee was now considered by the world to be "That Great Captain," possessed of "more of the loftiest virtues and power of humanity" than any other military leader in the world's history. The state government of Alabama announced proudly in a teacher's handbook that "now all the world yields him homage as one of the greatest men in history."

Occasionally, however, a southern writer missed the changes that had occurred in Lee's national status. The case of Thomas Nelson Page bears a special importance. If anyone should have been able to grasp the changing national mood toward the South, it should have been Page. As one of the most powerful southern literary figures of the late nineteenth century, Page had fared well by pitching his writings to a northern book and magazine market. In nonfiction works such as *The Old Dominion,* novels such as *Red Rock,* and the collection of short stories *In Ole Virginia,* he had described a South pleasing to the northern ear. There was no sectional animosity or attempts to justify the Rebel stance. Amid some romantic escapism, good for the literary market of that day, Page inserted themes of a sense of reunion, and of the tragedy of southern men of good principles, especially Virginians, caught up in forces beyond their control.

But Page's adoration of Lee got the better of him in the 1909 biography. *Robert E. Lee, the Southerner* smacked of the old Reconstruction era style of writing Confederate history. There was, for example, little material on Lee's personal character, or his postwar contributions to national reunion. Old, tired themes were plied instead, such as Lee's military greatness and his chivalric manner.

Page was lambasted for this anachronism. Important here was the assessment of a reviewer in *Nation*, who wrote that Page's biography would be admirable "if it might be judged by the canons of fiction." A chastised Page went back to the writer's table and revised his biography. Three years later he reissued it as *Robert E. Lee: Man and Soldier*, with changes the author made admittedly because of the "attractiveness" of the subject. Page's first effort had allotted only 39 pages to Lee's character and postwar exploits; the revised version contained 120 pages on these subjects. Now a reviewer in *Nation* described the book as an "apparently accurate account" and praised Page's "special contribution" of noting that "the greatness of Lee's character" resulted from the "admirable qualities" of his Virginia environment.

The Page episode tells much about the changing status of Robert E. Lee's image. Lee's national appeal after 1900 was as a man of great character, torn between love for the Union and his Virginia roots. Page's original 1909 biography was written in the context of a much older image, that of the postwar generation of writers of the Lost Cause.

Within a decade after his death, this first generation of postwar writers had centered their justification upon Robert E. Lee. Whatever their maudlin, one-dimensional approach to the Confederacy, one must give a generation of Jubal Earlys its due. In a near frenzy of writings in the two decades after Lee's death, they elevated him to the plane of a southern demigod.

It is important to remember that it was their private war. By 1900 the Jubal Earlys were anachronisms, even among their own southern brethren. This passing generation of early Confederate writers still fought out the tired, bitter sectional issues in pitiful veterans' magazines while other southerners basked in the new national praise accorded to Robert E. Lee. Early and his comrades still wrote of Lee as the invincible military chieftain, blamed James Longstreet for the loss at Gettysburg, and damned his Republican sentiments, and still viewed Yankee soldiers as a mongrel race who possessed overwhelming numbers but little virtue.

Meanwhile other southerners looked on proudly as Longstreet was a guest of honor at the inauguration of Theodore Roosevelt, and an honored dignitary at the centennial observance of the United States Military Academy. And while Jubal Early and his passing generation still wrote of Robert E. Lee as the invincible southern war chief, a new generation of Dixie writers spoke of new themes—Lee the American, the man of noble character, the dedicated public servant who loved the Union.

This was the description of Lee that won over the nation after 1900. It did not arise from the polemics of that first angry generation of Confederate writers after Appomattox. Their Lee was something else, fashioned for their own needs. He was a symbol of goodness for them also, but it was a degree of righteousness beyond human achievement, a stainless Christ symbol. Lee was an invincible Rebel god of war, who faltered in battle only when others failed him, and fell only to the bullish numbers thrown against him by General Ulysses Grant. Lee was good breeding and aristocratic lineage, the flower of a chivalric line that early admirers traced back to the Battle of Hastings.

The new Lee of 1907—the Lee inducted into the Hall of Fame and praised by every American president—was something quite different. He was the man of good character and intention—if sometimes misdirected, as in 1861. He was the man of basic American values of decency, duty, and honor, the devotee of unionism trapped in 1861 by conflicting loyalties. Lee was the postwar nationalist, driven by an unswerving determination to help restore the old Union.

The reasons for Virginia's dominance of southern letters in the late nineteenth century, and why the national reading audience was so enamored of the Old Dominion, are matters that have been described already. Important here is that these things did happen, and in the process, an image of Robert E. Lee—and the Confederacy—appeared that was totally unlike the image described by the earlier generation of Confederate authors.

There is much irony in this new portrayal of Lee that did much to help promote a sense of national reunion after 1900. Some observers have described the new group of southern authors as "romantics." Their treatment of Lee, however, involved no stereotyped romanticism, but was a convincing double-edged thrust of romance and tragedy. The earlier body of Lost Cause writers had pounded their fists in anguish against the growing American faith in pragmatism and in Social Darwinism's faith that the fittest institutions survive.

The new breed of southern writers found a skillful weapon in Social Darwinism. At once Lee was the epitome of romance and tragedy, as was the entire Confederacy. He remained the cavalier, bred in an idyllic society capable of producing superior men. Yet this same romantic environment that taught Lee the higher virtues of honor and duty became his undoing. Lee was no less tragic than romantic, trapped in an environment of agrarian capitalism and slaves. Thus his decision of 1861 to fight for the South was not something to be condemned. Criticize the environment, if one must, but praise Lee's devotion to his duty as a Virginian. So, despite his opposition to secession and slavery, Lee sorrowfully left Arlington and rode southward. Four years later, after Appomattox, that same devotion to principle moved Lee to work at mending the Union's scars by his example and counsel.

Here is the absolute irony of the Lost Cause. The vindication of the Confederacy rested heavily upon its supreme hero, and in the process, Robert E. Lee was robbed of much of his southernism. The elevation of his character to such a lofty position denied to him passions and inconsistencies usually attributed to the enigmatic southern mind.

Amid a South filled with paradox, Lee became steady and predictable, governed by a simple code of duty. In a land renowned for excess in war, politics, religion, and morality, Lee became the temperate soul of moderation in everything. He was the quiet churchman amid comrades filled with evangelical zeal; the gentle enemy who allegedly spoke of the Union foe as "those people" while others hurled epithets; the Confederate titan who shunned military trappings while others strutted in gold braid.

Examine the image of Robert E. Lee as it was developed by influential authors in the era of his birthday centennial, and it appears very nonsouthern. Robert E. Lee, Jr.'s *Recollections and Letters of Robert E. Lee*, which received a tremendous national ovation after its 1904 publication, was no saga of the elder Lee as a Rebel soldier—or even a southerner. The younger Lee centered upon the romance-tragedy themes, concentrated upon his father's character and nationalism. There were no chapter titles such as "Gettysburg," but an abundance on themes of "An Ideal Father" or "An Adviser of Young Men."

The other most persuasive Lee biographer of the era reiterated these themes. Charles Francis Adams was the most important nonsouthern voice of the new image. Adams' 1907 Lee centennial address at Washington and Lee University has been regarded by some historians as the climax of reconciliation between North and South. The invitation came after Adams had championed Lee in several important speeches and books, including *Lee at Appomattox and Other Essays; The Confederacy and the Transvaal: A People's Obligation to Robert E. Lee;* and *Shall Cromwell Have a Statue?*

In his famous Washington and Lee speech, as in these earlier writings and addresses, Adams deprived Lee of his southern nature. Adams translated the romance-tragedy rationale into the twin themes of character and nationalism. Lee's greatness—duty, honor, and loyalty to his people—were products of his environment. The tragedy was that in 1861 a grief-stricken Lee was entrapped by his upbringing. His adherence to the duty principle warred against his strong devotion to the Union. Although Lee chose duty, he should be praised for helping to save the Union, by virtue of his demeanor after Appomattox.

Here was the beginning of the modern Lee image. Lee has become not southern at all, lacking the excesses that characterize his region. His national stature emerged as a complement to the new American middle class. In his thoughtful study, *The Hero in American Society*, Dixon Wecter observed that Middle America demands of its heroes traits such as character, balance, and traditional virtues of hard work and the judicious use of power. Wecter concluded that the common ingredient of that highest tier of our hero symbols is the well-proportioned life, with nothing done in excess. One may be a military hero but no warlord, intelligent but not an intellectual, religious but no pious exhorter. The new Lee image meshed well with these demands.

Nor has the Lee image been altered in successive generations. The outpouring of writing in the southern renascence of the 1920s and 1930s failed to alter Lee's nonsouthern image. A new tide of national interest in the old Confederacy took many approaches: the new genre of romantic Old South films produced by Hollywood; the popularity of southern romantic novelists such as Stark Young and Francis Griswold; the amazing success of *Gone With the Wind;* and a flurry of new historical writings on the Confederacy. Not without reason did *Saturday Review* editor Bernard DeVoto complain that Dixie lost the war but was winning the renascence.

Even the greatest Confederate writer of that age, Douglas Southall Freeman, denied to Lee much of his southern background. Freeman's masterpiece, the four-volume *R. E. Lee*, saw him as a separatist Virginian, not a southerner. By Freeman's interpretation, Lee in secession and war was in many ways unlike his Deep South compatriots. He disliked slavery, abhorred secession, and possessed a deeper respect of the Union than did most Confederates. Examine Freeman's analysis closely, and the twin themes emerge that were stated by the late nineteenth-century Virginia local colorists. He was the cavalier, the flower of a superior Virginia culture that bred men of noble ideals. Lee was also the tragic hero, entrapped in 1861 by culture and principle, who later reasserted his strong nationalism after the surrender.

More important, Freeman saw Lee as a model of that steadiness admired by Middle America. Freeman's notable concluding chapter, "The Pattern of a Life," finds no excesses of character or temperament. There were no "dark currents." Lee was the personification of moderation in temper, dress, religion, personality, and every other adornment of the human soul. Freeman concluded that no mystery clouded the image of this man, who was guided only by simple religious faith and an awareness of good breeding.

Freeman stood atop a virtual mountain of literature on Lee, the Confederacy, and southern culture written in the 1930s. Buried somewhere in this mountain was an important but often unnoticed essay by the southern literary critic and poet Donald Davidson. A member of the original Fugitive group at Vanderbilt University, Davidson had established a reputation as a protector of regionalism. He became one of the Vanderbilt Agrarians, he was one of the Twelve Southerners who wrote

I'll Take My Stand, and he was author of other essays and books defending southern values.

Davidson's concern for preserving the South's customs surfaced again in an essay titled "A Note on American Heroes," published in the *Southern Review*. He complained that the South, in its haste to reassume a role in the mainstream of American society, had surrendered its hero images to the nation. Ever ready to please, southern exhorters had diluted their hero symbols to fit a bland national mold.

Davidson viewed Robert E. Lee as the supreme example of surrender. To appease the North, southern writers had altered his real nature. Lee had been transformed into the "milder, more yielding Lee, the college president and the quietist."

Donald Davidson remained the proverbial John the Baptist, crying alone in the wilderness. For over three decades, even southern authors had preached the image of Lee the nationalist. And in Davidson's own time, Douglas Freeman sealed the matter in his classic study, finally appraising Lee as little more than a catalog of those well-proportioned virtues demanded of heroes by Middle America. Somewhere in these generations of image building, the South lost touch with Robert E. Lee. Even if southerners doubted the abstraction of the national symbolism, they accepted it, or at least allowed it to cloud their vision of Lee as a regional entity. Gone was the Lee who once owned slaves, who even in 1861 spoke of a "cruel North" that possessed "evil designs." Absent from the predominant imagery was the hot-tempered general who once ordered the execution of a forager who had stolen a pig, who lapsed into what one of his staff members described as his "savage moods," and who in the years after Appomattox spoke angrily of the "vindictiveness and malignity of the Yankees."

To suggest that Lee was an exaggeration of southern traits has little, if anything to do with slavery, secession, or the Confederate experience. It refers instead to Lee's exhibiting of southern traits, a fact that has been obscured by his American image.

The southern mind has frustrated and intrigued observers for generations. At least in the twentieth century, the behavior and thought processes of southerners have ranked with slavery, race relations, and the Civil War as among the most discussed topics related to Dixie. Novelists, historians, literary critics, sociologists, theologians, and others have toiled to establish something concrete out of the intangibles of the southern character.

The three decades since 1950 in particular have witnessed a rush to the conference table. Symposiums and seminars by the hundreds—if not thousands—have groped with topics such as "The Idea of the South." National attention has been focused upon these introspective attempts to dissect the modern South and discover the characteristics, both good and bad, that make Dixie unique. The civil rights crisis, economic growth of the sunbelt, national conversion to the southern fundamentalism of Billy Graham, new Dixie influence in national politics, the mystique of the good ol' boy in American popular culture—all are part of the newest New South. John Egerton observed in *The Americanization of Dixie* that the current interest in the southern mind may reflect a fear that distinctive regional qualities are fast disappearing beneath the sprawl of Atlanta and the sprouting of fast-food establishments in every southern hamlet.

One is inclined to agree with Egerton, but to suggest there is nothing new in this. It is inherent in the southerner's concept of linear time to be conscious of what Allen Tate described as "the backward glance," and to view simultaneously the past and the menace of the present and the future. The sense of a mission to describe things characteristically southern is an old one. The Vanderbilt Agrarians and others felt this compulsion during the renascence era of the 1930s; they were fearful that the peculiarities of an agrarian culture would disappear beneath modernity. The "backward glance" characterized as well the local colorists, such as Thomas Nelson Page and Joel Chandler Harris, who strove to describe a civilization vanquished by the industrial revolution. Even the angry rebel authors of the Inner Lost Cause in the years immediately after the war, often expressed their commitment to eulogize the Old South before it disappeared from memory. It would appear that in a century of writing and oratory, the southern character has virtually been "talked to death." Ironically, no agreement has emerged from all of this discussion, and the resulting confusion resembles the proverb of the blind men and the elephant. Instead of finding consensus, one who seeks the roots of the southern mind is still confronted with widely varying viewpoints. At once white southerners in particular have been described as: dominated by racial superiority; obsessed with guilt; reverent of nature; wasteful of the land; hospitable; distrustful of outsiders; individualistic; easily led by group action; violent; chivalrous; hedonistic; possessed of deep piety; lazy; restless; home-loving.

All of this is not as contradictory as it appears. Leaving aside the question of racial attitudes, almost everything in this listing could be taken as offspring of four root characteristics of the traditional white southern mind. Here one observes a society *alienated* from the main currents of American myth and faith. Some of this alienation had come out of that peculiar *classical-Christian mentality* that produced a distinct view of the tragedy of the never-changing human condition. Simultaneously, the southern mind has raced wildly between *extremes*—intense piety and sensuality, genial hospitality and violence, a high rate of illiteracy and a notable regional literature, reverence for order and resentment for authority, and numerous other apparent contradictions. In truth these are not contradictions at all, but are elements of that underlying *paradox* in the southern character.

Certainly any full description of the southern character would include other traits. Yet these four—alienation, a classical-Christian thought process, extremism, and paradox—appear consistently in analyses of the mind of the South by modern observers. And one observes them—often to excess—in the life of Robert E. Lee.

Southerners have been for generations an alienated people, divorced from the mainstream of the American faith. Some of this alienation was there before the Civil War, in slavery, the plantation economy, and the intellectual isolation of the planter class. The remainder came with defeat in the Civil War, which insured that the region would remain apart from the American ideals of success and plenty.

The myths are known well to students of southern culture. C. Vann Woodward, in *The Burden of Southern History* recalled the importance of the national doctrine of success, a creed brought to the New World in the puritan faith. Somehow the Enlightenment of the eighteenth century failed to diminish the credo that success, material or otherwise, is a sign of Jehovah's grace. Instead, victory in the American Revolution and survival in the War of 1812 gave succor to the myth. By the early nineteenth century, the American faith was that of success. After the Civil War, acceptance of Social Darwinism sealed the issue. The fittest institutions survive, and Dixie perished in the trenches before Richmond.

All of this came down hard upon a defeated South. Perhaps there was a measure of guilt in the southern postwar consciousness because the region had sundered the old Union and had fought against the American flag. However, the deeper sense of guilt was probably due to surrender, not secession. The South suffered something unique in the national experience—

total defeat and military conquest. The Confederacy had failed to inherit the American legacy of success and achievement. Given the nature of southern piety's reliance upon the closeness of man and God, defeat implied alienation not only from the American dream, but from the very shadow of the Almighty. It is heretical enough to suggest that Robert E. Lee also was the alienated southerner, because this image runs counter to his symbol as Lee the American. So here the architects of Lee's national image downplayed the obvious—that he *was* the foremost leader of a rebellion against the flag he had served for three decades, and led an army fashioned by men who desired to preserve human slavery and rend the Union asunder permanently.

When Appomattox ended those hopes, Lee shared also the denial of the American dreams of success and prosperity. Lee for a lifetime idolized George Washington and had married the granddaughter of that patriot's adopted son. Now Robert Lee was the ex-Rebel, who was deprived of his citizenship and threatened with prosecution for treason. He was the paroled prisoner, forced to give an oath of allegiance to an America that believed increasingly that victory was the test of good causes.

Denied to Lee as well was the dream of American prosperity. His wife's legacy of Arlington had fallen beneath the auctioneer's gavel during wartime. Lee accumulated little wealth; in fact, one is hardpressed to uncover a single foot of land ever obtained by Lee himself. Even many of his subordinates in the Army of Northern Virginia spent their last years on their own ground—Wade Hampton on his Carolina estate, James Longstreet on his Georgia farm, and Richard Ewell on his wife's lands in Tennessee. Lee's last five years after Appomattox were spent in a modest borrowed home in Lexington, Virginia—a long way from the grandeur of Arlington, and even farther from Camelot.

But this had been the pattern of a life. Robert E. Lee not only failed to share in the American dream, but seemed alienated as well from the mainstream of the southern planter class. He was never part of the plantation legend and, in fact, lived most of his life on the fringe of that facet of greatness of the Lee family. Much has been made of his birth at Stratford, ancestral home of many well-known eighteenth-century statesmen, such as Richard Bland Lee, Arthur Lee, and Francis Lightfoot Lee. Several score of writers have drawn upon the symbolism of Robert E. Lee's birth in the southeast bedroom where two signers of the Declaration of Independence were also brought into the world.

Yet Lee was the noninheritor, and his involvement in the noble traditions of Stratford lasted only four years. As a child he was a tenant in the mansion, allowed to reside there only because the first wife of his father was a cousin, Matilda Lee, heiress to Stratford Hall. She knew of the reckless financial schemes of Light-Horse Harry Lee and before her death in 1790 had placed Stratford Hall in trust to her children. In 1811 her son Henry, Robert's half-brother, claimed his inheritance, and Light-Horse Harry's family moved to Alexandria.

The new quarters were modest because Harry Lee's financial losses had left the family almost penniless. Some of Stratford Hall's furniture had been sold to pay his debts; despite this, before Robert Lee's second birthday his father had served two sentences in debtor's prison. Finally, in 1813 a disgraced Henry Lee, after suffering wounds in a Baltimore political riot, abandoned his family for self-imposed exile in Barbados.

The decline of Harry Lee, vaunted Revolutionary War cavalryman, Virginia governor, and advisor to George Washington, was symbolic of a larger decrease in the financial and political power of the Lees of the Stratford and Leesylvania clans. The golden era of eighteenth-century Virginia's tobacco aristocracy had passed, and so had the political impact of the Lee clan, witnessed once in the national stature of Richard Bland, Richard Henry, Francis Lightfoot, Arthur, Light-Horse Harry, and other Lees. Even Stratford disappeared from the family's grasp in 1820, after financial and moral disgrace by Robert's half-brother, Henry, sullied the Lee name again. Robert E. Lee's young life was a mosaic of nostalgia over a society he never really shared. His cousins—however distant—lived on estates along the Potomac, in the Northern Neck and on the Peninsula, such as Arlington, Ravensworth, Romancoke, White House, Kinloch, and many others. Some of these estates would be bequeathed to Lee's children, but only because they were the inheritance of his future wife, Mary Custis of Arlington. Meanwhile Lee lived with his invalid mother, Anne Carter, in the modest Alexandria home.

When he came of age, what was Robert Lee to do? He loved the Virginia land passionately; in fact, his often formal letters written home from military outposts in later years could wax poetic when Lee recalled his own memories of visiting family estates. But there was no plantation legacy for him, and no funds available to pursue a medical career, which had interested him. The expenses incurred in maintaining his older brother, Carter, at Harvard forbade Lee's enrollment in a better school. There is substantial evidence that Robert E. Lee elected for West Point and an army career because—given the family's financial circumstances—there was nowhere else for a gentleman to go.

So Lee became, as he described it more than once, a wanderer. For another three decades after graduation from the military academy in 1829, he moved from one army outpost to another. Much of this time was spent in the routine duties of an officer of engineers at assignments far from Lee's beloved Virginia, such as St. Louis and the humid Georgia coastal area.

Robert E. Lee's later prominence in the Civil War has obscured some formative matters in his earlier life. He appears to be a classic example of southern irony. Circumstances demanded that Lee spend many years of his life alienated from those things he loved best.

His lengthy correspondence with family and friends during these years has been well preserved in the Library of Congress, the Virginia Historical Society, and elsewhere. His many letters reveal an exaggerated case of that devotion to family, community, and the soil characteristic of most southerners. Particularly by the middle 1850s, Lee's letters exhibit an ever-growing frustration with absence from wife and children, gnawing homesickness for Virginia, and disappointment with tedious, routine life in army posts.

The irony is again unmistakable. Lee's memories of early years in Virginia focused upon the beauty and grandeur of Arlington, Ravensworth, and other palatial estates owned by relatives. He was removed from this society, and indeed was never part of it.

Lee also had been reared in the aura of the Lee name. Regardless of the tarnished reputation of Light-Horse Harry, he had enjoyed fame as a Revolutionary War hero, and as friend and confidant of George Washington. Robert Lee could remember that unforgettable day as a child when the Marquis De Lafayette had visited the modest home in Alexandria to pay respects to the widow and children of Harry Lee.

But for Robert Lee, a military career had involved slow promotion, modest pay, and usually routine service. His outstanding performance on Winfield Scott's staff in the Mexican War may have inspired the General's admiration, but little substantial came out of it. Not until 1855—after twenty-seven years of service—was Lee even promoted to lieutenant colonel. Evidently by the 1850s Lee considered his military career to be unsuccessful and spoke occasionally of resigning. An unfulfilled Robert Lee more than once exhorted his wife to be patient about his hopes for promotion. Once he glumly wrote "Do not give yourself any anxiety about the appointment. . . . You will be sure to be disappointed."

James H. Justus, in an essay "On the Restlessness of Southerners," suggested that the popular American image of the lazy, satisfied, sedentary citizen of Dixie has been overdone. Justus pointed to the counterbalance found in southern literature, which is rich with the symbolism of the restless, driven, unsatisfied Ishmael. The unfulfilled southerner is present in Erskine Caldwell's millworkers, Eudora Welty's King MacLain of *The Golden Apples*, William Faulkner's Temple Drake and Bayard Sartoris, and Thomas Wolfe's protagonist, Eugene Gant.

Before *Of Time and the River* was published, Thomas Wolfe confided to a friend that the book would concentrate on two matters that "haunt and hurt us: the eternal wandering, moving, questing, loneliness, homesickness, and the desire of the soul for a home, peace, fixity, repose." To Wolfe these were the essentials—"Of wandering forever and the earth again." He spoke of Eugene Gant, but the same alienation characterized the quest of Robert E. Lee.

Read his letters written before the Civil War, and the feeling of estranged wanderer comes through strongly. Apparently Lee steadily fashioned a self-image as a nomad, destined to live out a restless life separated from his roots. To Lee, his army life "debars all hope of domestic enjoyment," and he viewed absences from his wife and children as "a just punishment for my sins." Steadily "my departures grow harder to bear with years," and once he grieved for his absent children, and mourned "probably they and I will never meet again."

Lee did return home permanently to Virginia in 1861, but the irony of his alienation did not cease. For he came back to fight for a southern oligarchy of which he was never a part. He detested secession and spoke in contempt of the lower South aristocracy, which he believed had brought the South to the brink of war. Despite his occasional possession of a slave, Lee considered slavery to be a malignant institution. Here is the irony of Robert Lee becoming the principal standard-bearer of the Confederacy, the most prominent Rebel general of a cause he never represented.

Lee's decision in 1861 to resign from the United States Army and fight for Virginia has become part of the American canon of folklore and heroism. His grief in this decision has been described as surpassing the travail of other good men forced to make the fateful choice between blue and gray.

No one would deny that Robert Lee's decision was heart-wrenching. Allegiance with the South involved more than the severance of an army career which spanned over three decades, and the potential loss of his wife's estate at Arlington. Lee for a lifetime stood in awe of his absolute hero, George Washington. The 1861 decision must have stirred troubled thoughts of how he now would participate in the destruction of the Union that Washington, his own father, and others had worked to perfect.

Yet immediately after his momentous decision on April 20, 1861, Robert E. Lee threw himself into the southern war effort. Three days later, without waiting for his resignation to be accepted by the United States government, Lee accepted command of Virginia's forces. Immediately he began vigorous war preparations, weeks before Virginia's citizens had opportunity to vote on the secession ordinance.

Even the transformation in Lee's vocabulary was striking. Once he had spoken of secession as "nothing but revolution," and could see "no greater calamity" than the dissolution of the Union. In a January, 1861, letter to his cousin, "Markie" Williams, Lee had described the idea of a southern republic as a "folly," and said he wished to live under no other government but the United States.

Yet soon after his April decision, Lee would speak of "the evil designs of the North." The Union had become "a cruel enemy" making war against a Rebel cause "sacred and worthy."

Indeed, as early as July of 1861, Lee promised to fight for the Confederate cause "as long as there is one horse that can carry his rider and one arm that can wield a sword."

Robert E. Lee probably saw no inconsistency in this rapid conversion from the sorrowful Unionist to the ardent Confederate. In fact he may have never pondered the matter. In essence he was a nonreasoning individual who abdicated decisions to forces beyond his control. By the 1850s his pattern of life was well established—to move almost mechanically, governed by the unseen force of Divine Providence and an unswerving devotion to his concept of duty. Later Lee explained how his thought processes affected his Civil War generalship: "I think and work with all my power to bring the troops to the right place at the right time; then I have done my duty. As soon as I order them into battle, I leave my army in the hands of God."

In this, Lee was an exaggeration of the classical-Christian mentality that is another signal trait of the southern mind. Critic Robert Heilman, in his essay on the southern temper, spoke of that basic distrust of analysis, that fear that too much introspection would threaten the whole cloth. The whole cloth was belief in the permanent existence of good and evil.

One root of the nonanalytical approach of the mind of the South was the classical-Christian mentality of antebellum Dixie. The fascination with Greek Revival architecture, law as an exalted profession, and Ciceronian rhetoric underlay a basic classical-Christian view of life. It was partly a classical love for fixed order, but also a pietistic approach to the Great Chain of Being.

In brief, the southern mind disclaimed infinite progress and strove to accept a mixture of good and evil in one's existence. Salvation was not perfection, but was an accord that acknowledged the verities of righteousness and evil. Such a view sprang not from the Enlightenment, but from seventeenth-century puritanism. It accepted things as they were, established limitations on progress, and committed one to the awareness of Divine Providence in everyday life. It is a commitment to noncommitment, an ambivalent Hamlet complex that tempers individuality with faith in the intervention of the Creator in human affairs.

By the 1850s, Robert E. Lee had become an exaggeration of this classical-Christian view. Lee's correspondence indicates that his frustrations and concerns were multiple. He was absent frequently from a semi-invalid wife, and feared for the training of his children during long absences. Lee had become unhappy in a career that provided scant rewards in promotion, and which kept him away from Virginia. He appeared to have an extreme view of his own humanity, fearful perhaps that he would duplicate the failures of Light-Horse Harry Lee.

Lee's response to these self-conscious imperfections in his life was a retreat. He withdrew into a code of duty and faith in Divine Providence, into an exaggerated form of that southern acknowledgment of the presence of evil or failure.

It was almost a classical acknowledgment of the presence of tragedy. Robert Lee grasped the dichotomy between ambition and station in life, and then strove to make peace with the question of why he did not share in the American dream of success. It implied an acceptance of failure—or at least unhappiness, and this attitude was characteristically southern. One wonders whether the nonreasoning process—this commitment to duty and providence—became for Lee an opiate.

Perhaps Lee's nonanalytical approach left him unaware of his possession of another southern trait. For generations writers have emphasized Lee's reserve, steadiness, and dignified bearing. The image of the simplistic, consistent Lee emerged in postwar biographies by such as the Reverend John William Jones's *Personal Reminiscences, Anecdotes and Letters of General Robert E. Lee,* Jones's volume, later to be used by many Lee biographers as a source book, was hailed by the contemporary *Southern Magazine* as "a household book in all Southern homes." In chapters with titles such as "Modest Humility, Simplicity and Gentleness," the writer portrayed the General as temperate in all of life's affairs.

This image underlay the symbolism of Robert E. Lee's national hero status after 1900. Lee, the Middle American without excesses, was the focus of the writings of the 1900–1910 era. Later, in the 1930s, Douglas Southall Freeman centered his appraisal of the General upon this same principle.

Yet Lee can appear as well an extremist, the product of a southern culture with apparent contradictions. Temperance has never been a virtue below the Potomac. The extremes are present even in the most simple observations of geography— the lush, verdant Shenandoah Valley and the barren, sterile expanses of central Alabama, the cool and lofty peaks of Tennessee's Unaka Mountains, and the sweltering bottomlands surrounding Memphis.

The mental processes of southern people are just as extreme. Here is the heart of American religious fundamentalism and the perennial nation-leader in statistics of homicides and aggravated assault. Serious observers have spoken of an ease and congeniality in the Dixie nature and a humanistic approach to one's personal dealings with his fellow man. Yet one South Carolina county in the 1960s boasted a murder rate exceeding that of the entire British Isles. Nashville, Tennessee, is the headquarters for the huge, conservative Southern Baptist Church and the Church of Christ and is headquarters of the Methodist Publishing House. One-third of the property in Davidson County—Metropolitan Nashville—is tax-exempt for religious purposes. Long regarded as the capital of the Bible Belt, Nashville also possesses a high rate of homicides and a serious record of drug abuse.

The extremes appear almost endless in southern behavior.

The South is a land that has produced Will Campbell and Ross Barnett, Chapel Hill and Bob Jones University, William Faulkner and Roy Acuff. Here is a tradition of disrespect for authority and evasion of the law commingled with one hundred percent Americanism. The same Dixie statesmen who damned the central government's excessive powers and shared George Wallace's appraisal of Washington bureaucracy condemned others who rejected that government's war policies in Vietnam.

Robert E. Lee was not immune from the role of southerner as extremist. In fact, in this—as in matters of alienation and the classical-Christian outlook, Lee appears an exaggeration of the southern norm. Almost everything he did was carried out in the extreme. There is a radical element in the intensity of his abstemious habits, humility, modesty, and other personal habits. Lee's letters and other personal papers exhibit a concern with principles such as duty and self-denial that is excessive, if not obsessive.

Despite his image as a soul of moderation, much that Lee did appeared the opposite. For example, there was his enduring concern for the moral training of his children during long absences in prewar military service. For years he wrote them long preachments on behavior in documents that were more sermons than letters from a father. In the 1850s, growing belief in the outside workings of Divine Providence had come by the 1860s to be pervasive in all of his actions. Thus in 1861, when a plan of attack failed during the campaign in western Virginia, Lee explained that "the Ruler of the Universe willed otherwise, and sent a storm to disconcert the well-laid plan." A simple Christian faith in hopes for a more satisfying life after death was transformed into a nearly morbid sense of other-worldness, that man's lot on earth was doomed to unhappiness. So after he read the funeral service for a child who had died at a dusty Texas outpost, Lee exhorted his wife, that it was better for the child to die "in innocence," because he "has been saved from sin and

misery here." When the casualty lists from the battle of First
Bull Run arrived in Richmond, Lee urged her again to grieve
not for the dead, but for their remaining friends and relatives,
since "The former are at rest. The latter must suffer."

Above all, there was the matter of Robert E. Lee's great self-
control. Apparently he did possess a strong temper, of which he
was well aware. Once he cautioned a staff member, "When I
lose my temper, don't let it make you angry." On another occasion, he became angry at a visitor to his camp, and later
stormed at another staff member, "Why did you permit that
man to come to my tent and make me show my temper?"
There were also times of an angry depression, described by
an aide as "one of his savage moods," when his staff officers
thought "it was safer to keep out of his way."

But on most occasions Robert E. Lee masked a stormy inner
nature beneath a mantle of almost practiced self-control. His
obsession with this noble quality became evident in the 1850s.
It pervaded his correspondence to wife and children and was a
prominent subject in his diary notes written during the six
years before the outbreak of the Civil War.

Lee's devotion to the code of self-control probably was rooted
in several factors. Not long before his death, he admitted that
he practiced the habit of self-discipline extensively. A former
student at Washington College recalled that Lee explained to
him that while one initially would find it difficult "to control
the operation of your mind" under all circumstances, that it
could be done by practice and determination. Lee added that
had it not been for this power, "I do not see how I could have
stood what I had to go through with."

Even in waging war, Robert E. Lee appears as the extremist.
On one hand, here was the Christian soldier of kind spirit, un-
pretentious demeanor, and a deep religious faith. He said his
prayers faithfully in camp, talked with colleagues about spiritual matters, and spoke often of his desire for God's will to be

done. Yet Lee fell upon the northern Philistines with a ferocity unequaled among the Confederate leadership. Battle seemed to exhilarate Lee. One staff officer remarked later that "General Lee in a drawing room was a very different man from General Lee in the field." The English observer Francis Lawley spoke of how Lee's very appearance changed in combat, and remembered "his flashing eyes and sternly-set lips . . . the light of battle still flaming in his eyes."

This was quite another Lee, who combined aggressiveness, audacity, and an absolute determination to crush the enemy. This was the Lee of Fredericksburg, who watched the slaughter of Union troops and mused, "It is well that war is so terrible— we would grow too fond of it." Years later Lee was still a puzzle to his famous artillery officer, General Edward Porter Alexander. Alexander noted that no one could meet Robert E. Lee without being impressed by "his dignity of character . . . and his calm self-reliance." Under the surface, however, there was also "the existence of such phenomenal audacity."

In war as he had been in peace, Robert E. Lee was a paradox of extremes. He was the advocate of the Union who led an army of secessionists; and the man who described slavery as "a moral and political evil" but who fought for the slavocracy. Lee was one of almost incredible gentleness, Christian piety, and sensitivity for the feelings of others. He was also the greatest artist of violence possessed by the Confederacy, and a man whose calm spirit could be transformed into high excitement by battle.

Lee is the greatest paradox of a paradoxical South. There is much irony in this, just as one can view in Lee's embodiment of a sense of alienation, a classical-Christian mentality and extremism. Bruce Catton's observation that Lee is still "one of the most profound enigmas of American life" could apply to southern Americans most of all.

The symbolism inherent in Robert E. Lee's national image

has obscured the presence in him of these distinctive features of the southern mind. Lee has in some ways remained unreal to the South that idolizes him. He has remained as well apart, with a chasm separating Lee's middle-class image from the excesses of his own people. In part because of this, the South has never understood him well.

The irony is that Robert E. Lee was so much like his fellow southerners, and perhaps the closeness and the intensity of the common traits have also clouded the vision of those southerners who revere him. Lee appears an exaggeration of an exaggerated society. The enigmas in Lee's nature support the thesis that a hero is an aberration of the society that ennobled him. Once enshrined, his nature has become obscured.

Chapter Four

THE ENDURING MEMORY

Over a century later, the Civil War remains the absolute catalyst and trauma of the southern heritage. The number of young men lost in Confederate ranks was ghastly enough. Almost 300,000 Rebel soldiers perished from wounds or disease. In the cold analysis of casualty statistics, compared to American deaths in Vietnam, the figure is catastrophic. The fact that five times as many southerners died in the Civil War as did Americans in Vietnam is only the surface reality. More horrible is the realization that, in terms of the population of 1860, and 1960, one of every nineteen white southerners perished in the war, whereas only 1 of every 3,050 Americans was killed in Southeast Asia.

The killing and maiming of virtually an entire generation of southern men was accompanied by even more lasting damage. Billions of dollars of losses in agriculture, industry, railroads and commerce caused a near economic castration from which the South has not recovered. The social and racial readjustments consequent to the freeing of 3.5 million slaves endure as well. Culturally, the South would remain provincial and at best second-rate until the tide began changing in the renascence of the 1920s and 1930s. Even more enduring has been the long memory of defeat, that state of dwelling in what Robert Penn Warren described as the "City of the Soul." The Lost Cause was far more than the fantasies and bitter rhetoric of aging Confederate soldiers, or the statues erected on southern courthouse squares by white-haired ladies from local memorial societies.

The Lost Cause was a realization of mortality existing in an America that reached for the gnostic immortal; it was an admission of failure juxtaposed against national faith in success and achievement. Defeat reinforced belief in that distinctive southern piety that was grounded in adherence to the God of the Old Testament, who intervened in human affairs, blessed the righteous, and punished the transgressor. This time Jehovah had aided the Philistines, and the Israelites of the demolished Confederacy were troubled by guilt and a sense of estrangement.

Still, one of the greatest of these paradoxes has been the attitude towards the Civil War expressed in several avenues of southern culture. In critical areas of modern serious literature and in the popular arts, the Civil War has received second-class treatment. The irony is two-fold. Here is a land rich in musical tradition, oral communication and modern literary talent which finds difficulty in expressing with depth the great tragedy of southern history.

Certainly there has been no dearth of writings on the Confederacy. Over a thousand Civil War novels have been written by southerners. Dixie poets have treated the war in poems that may run into the tens of thousands. The number of nonfiction works on the war is almost incalculable. Surely the total number of books, articles, essays, printed orations, pamphlets, and other literature must run into the hundreds of thousands.

A sizable amount of this writing came out of two great outpourings of Civil War writing in the twentieth century. Certainly one would have expected that the literature of the southern renascence would have explored the Civil War in depth. The flourishing of literary talent in the two decades before the Second World War has been discussed laboriously by critics, historians, and other observers. Poet Allen Tate's description of the perspective of southern writers in that peculiar era—the "backward glance"—has been quoted in scores of books.

Few would contest that the southern generation of writers between the two world wars did benefit from a special perspective of time and place. The world of William Faulkner, Eudora Welty, and Caroline Gordon *was* two-dimensional. These writers lived in the last generation that saw the Confederate veteran as a reality, and experienced the last vestiges of the South as a diminishing agrarian empire. Yet they saw also the first growth of that commercial and cultural Americanization of Dixie that troubled the Twelve Southerners in *I'll Take My Stand.*

The result was a flowering of regional literary talent between 1920 and 1940 that some critics speculate can never be repeated. Here was the fiction of William Faulkner, Thomas Wolfe, Eudora Welty, and Erskine Caldwell, the poetry of Allen Tate, John Crowe Ransom, and Donald Davidson, and the nonfiction writer Douglas Southall Freeman. Freeman, the historian and journalist, editor of the Richmond *News Leader,* is mentioned as a solitary entry in the nonfiction category for good reason. It is ironic that despite the brilliant display of regional letters of the renascence years, so little of it explored the Confederacy in depth. Freeman, however, achieved this in his Pulitzer Prize-winning biography *R. E. Lee.*

Despite the prolific amount of "pure" historical writing on the Confederacy in this era, one is hard-pressed to find equals to Freeman. Certainly the quantity of work was there, in an outpouring of books and articles not to be duplicated until the centennial years. In the thirteen years prior to Pearl Harbor, thirteen biographies of Robert E. Lee, five of Jefferson Davis, and two of Nathan Bedford Forrest were issued. In fact, during this same period, almost six hundred biographies of southerners were issued in either book or pamphlet form. Yet few of these writings display deep insight into the Confederacy. Obviously the historians of the renascence years labored without the fringe benefits of xerox, microfilm, computers, and hefty federal research grants. Yet they possessed the advantage of what Professor Lewis Simpson described as "the recovery of memory and history" in that they benefited from a peculiar inspiration of a sense of time and place.

Still, the quality of the numerous historical works on the Confederacy written by southerners during the renascence years is disappointing. Frank Owsley wrote about the Civil War, but he belongs to the latter generation of the 1940s along with Bell Wiley and Robert Selph Henry. Given that magnificent perspective of bearing witness to the last vestiges of one South and the development of another, the paucity of insight by native writers is striking.

The poetry and fiction of the renascence display this same lack of absolute insight into the South in the Civil War. No epic of the Confederacy matches Stephen Vincent Benet's "John Brown's Body." Allen Tate's "Ode to the Confederate Dead" and Donald Davidson's "Lee in the Mountains" were splendid pieces, but they deal with the aftermath, not the war itself. Tate's protagonist is the watcher at the gate, whose sentiments are caught between the moldering gravestones of Rebels and his own presence in the twentieth century. Davidson's central figure is not the Lee of the war years, but the weary, aging college president who gazes upon the Blue Ridge Mountains and ponders whether the postwar South would have fared differently had he fled there with his diminishing army in 1865.

Even the hallmark of the renascence years—the brilliant outpouring of fiction by southern authors—displays an unwillingness to cope with the Confederate epoch. Some sixty novels relating to the Civil War were written by southern writers during this period. Among them were the most well-known fictions about the Civil War. It was the age of Stark Young's *So Red the Rose*, Andrew Lytle's *The Long Night*, Caroline Gordon's *None Shall Look Back*, Allen Tate's *The Fathers*, William Faulkner's *The Unvanquished*, and Margaret Mitchell's international bestseller, *Gone With the Wind*.

Yet critic Louis Rubin, Jr., in his essay "The Image of an Army: The Civil War in Southern Fiction," has reminded us that even the best of these novels share common attributes with the thousand others written by Dixie authors since Appomattox. Even the best, Rubin suggests, fall short of a *War and Peace*. As Rubin observes, there is no great Confederate novel with a protagonist such as Pierre Bezukhov, to embody the southern mind at war, in which a character develops under the stress that his compatriots are enduring. Instead, as Rubin has argued convincingly, even the best southern war novels lack the great protagonist who relates the rise and fall of the Confederacy. In *Absalom, Absalom!*, Faulkner describes the war, but only in the context of a larger epic of the fortunes of the Sutpen family before and after Appomattox. Stark Young's *So Red the Rose* and Caroline Gordon's *None Shall Look Back* describe southerners in the war as representative of greater southern values unbridled by time and place. Other novels, such as *Gone With the Wind*, not only use the war as a device to exhibit southern traits, but are concerned more with the aftermath and not the conflict itself.

• Louis Rubin's argument is that southerners are too oriented to that intricate fabric of family, community, and history to do otherwise. Robert Lively in his study of Civil War novels, *Fiction Fights the Civil War*, observed the difference in treatment of the conflict by writers of the North and South. Southern authors of the renascence described the war in a broader social perspective. Grounded in a unique reference of family and community, they described the war in terms of the *group*, particularly its rise and decline. In contrast, Yankee writers, such as Stephen Crane, in his *The Red Badge of Courage*, centered upon the struggle of the individual.

Rubin's argument, of course, was that southern novelists were unable to become existentialists in their treatment of the Civil War. He suggested that any great war novel must do something that southern authors cannot achieve—to disengage from any time-and-place perspective, to exist without any past and future. Instead, Rubin argues, southern novelists view man as existing within a society, and they have in the main been unable to describe a central character divorced from time and place.

If one accepts Rubin's argument as valid, another trait of southern writing on the Civil War during the renascence possesses special meaning. Some of the most powerful literary comment was biography, when southerners, forced by the demands of the genre, *had* to concentrate upon the experiences of a single individual. One could point again to Douglas Freeman's masterpiece on Lee, to Allen Tate's life of "Stonewall" Jackson, and to Robert Penn Warren's study of Jefferson Davis. That much of the best Civil War writing coming from the renascence era was character study does add weight to Rubin's argument that southern writers, however talented, could not isolate an individual from time and place.

Even the trend towards existentialism in southern writing of the 1960s and 1970s has failed to produce the great Confederate iliad. Louis Rubin's comment on the inability of the southern writer to isolate a protagonist from space and time has been contradicted by the novels of Walker Percy, James Dickey, and William Styron. Percy's characters in *The Moviegoer, Love in the Ruins*, and in his other novels are void of a definite sense of place and past. James Dickey's *Deliverance* is a southern metaphor of the entire human condition. Jack Kirby observed in *Media-Made Dixie* that Dickey's tale of the ordeal of Atlanta suburbanites on an Appalachian river could have been set in any locale. Hence, Kirby observed that in *Deliverance* "the southerner is merely modern Everyman, without special attachments or insights from his soil and past."

Percy's and Dickey's novels have come shortly after a second huge surge of interest in Civil War writing which began in the late 1950s. The Civil War centennial of 1961–1965 was almost as great a tragedy as the war itself. The centennial was a tawdry display of commercialization wrapped in the banalities of self-righteous tones, in the hawking of merchandise, advertising, and the peddling of several hundred new books about the Civil War.

The centennial was a national experience, not a product of the southern memory. Even before 1961 a heavily commercialized surge of national interest in the war was obvious. Over sixty Civil War roundtables—most in nonsouthern urban areas—were functioning, as was the Confederate Research Club in England. The New York *Herald Tribune* began publication of a new comic strip "Johnny Reb and Billy Yank," while between 1959 and 1969, nearly two hundred doctoral dissertations on war topics were underway on university campuses.

Then in 1961 the war erupted in a commercial orgy. The Montgomery, Alabama, centennial group allotted $100,000 for the reenactment of the inauguration of Jefferson Davis. Nearly a quarter of this went to the John Rogers Producing Company of Ohio, which wrote and produced the script for a thousand-member cast, and advised on such details as fireworks. On the day of the reenactment, some twenty thousand people, many in period costumes, lined the hill to watch the preinauguration parade.

Meanwhile, the First Manassas Corporation staged the reenactment of Bull Run at an estimated cost of $200,000. Costumed units from twenty-three states participated. Nearly two hundred horses had been purchased and trained previously to be conditioned to gunfire produced by such "reactivated" units

as the Washington D.C. Blues. Journalist Harry Golden recalled a friend who was "killed" in the Manassas reenactment
and proceeded to die for his country in three later battles.

Businessmen had learned that means to capitalize upon the
nation's interest were legion. The National Civil War Centennial Commission even set up an advertising subcommit-
tee to aid businessmen in relating their products to the war.
Such advice was provided as: "Tobacco advertisers can point to
the clandestine barter in smoking and chewing tobacco that
brought enemy soldiers together." The Chrysler Corporation in
1961 began advertising a specially made Valiant, the "Dixie
Special" to be sold only in southern states; it featured a paint
finish of Confederate gray. Hammacher, Schlemmer and Company of New York offered a canine "turncoat" for poodles, one
side blue, the other gray. Revell, Incorporated, prepared a three-
foot scale model of the Confederate raider *Alabama*, while the
National Cap and Cloth Hat Institute prepared a Civil War cap
in a choice of colors. The Ravenel Tourist Agency of Charleston sold framed copies of the South Carolina secession ordinance for twenty-five dollars. An Atlanta radio station broadcast daily newscasts of the "latest" developments in various
war zones.

Even before the centennial began officially with the Fort
Sumter observance, the nation seemed bent on a commercial
juggernaut. Parker Brothers, of "Monopoly" fame, received
25,000 orders within a single week after its issuance of a new
board game titled "1863." Within five months after its publication in 1960, Doubleday's massive *American Heritage Picture History of the Civil War* sold 350,000 copies for twenty
dollars each—a record for a book in that price range. One television network scored heavily with a cavalier fantasia, "The
Gray Ghost," which dramatized the exploits of Confederate
cavalryman Colonel John Mosby. Another network cast aside
its "Riverboat" series and improved ratings with "The Ameri-

cans," a Civil War drama with the traditional situation plot of one brother wearing blue, the other gray. Meanwhile the Sinclair Oil Company allotted almost a quarter of a million dollars for an advertising campaign encouraging automobile trips to historic sites. Popular magazines were quick to take advantage of the financial possibilities of the centennial. Typical was the *Saturday Evening Post*'s inauguration of a series of "Untold Stories of the Civil War." The magazine promised readers that "commonplace, impersonal history" would be bypassed, in order to reveal "little-known, intimate aspects of that brave, tragic period." Amid snappy Madison Avenue language, the *Post* published such articles as "Blue and Gray Braves." The masthead promised readers a story of some ten thousand Indians who fought in the war, complete with tales of "their heroism—and their savagery."

Two meaningful things emerge from all the frenzy of the centennial era. First, it was not a southern celebration, but was a near national fad. The centennial was squarely in the tradition of American commemorative affairs, which exhaust themselves in a glut of overstatement, overexposure, and rampant commercialization. Forty-six state Civil War centennial commissions oversaw a broad range of activities: sponsoring essay contests; issuing books, filmstrips, and bulletins; erecting historical markers to call attention to war events; and many other projects. During the centennial, Civil War roundtables composed usually of professional and business people found their greatest popularity in northern cities. Since the general collapse of national interest in the Civil War in the 1960s, many of the roundtables in southern locales closed down operations. Meanwhile large, enthusiastic groups continue in Chicago, Milwaukee, Minneapolis, New York, and other nonsouthern cities.

A second characteristic of the era possesses even a deeper significance. What southerners did contribute to the great centennial pageant lacked fervor and depth of feeling commensurate with the war's importance to the region. The shallowness of battlefield reenactments illustrates this dearth of insight and retrospection. Such festivals were described by some observers as childish exercises, and by others as obstacles to the improvement of smoldering race relations in Dixie.

Even the most serious tangible contribution made by the South to the centennial often lacked—or appeared to miss—the deep meaning of the Confederate experience to the region. A sizable proportion of the seemingly endless number of centennial books were written by southerners, and most of these were superficial in quality. Every general, however lackluster and unimportant, who ever mounted a horse was accorded a biography. Southern archives and libraries, always rich in caches of documentary war sources were "raided" by professors, graduate students, hack writers, and others, who hastily published a stream of reminiscences, letters, and diaries. One editor complained that "the last surviving scraps" from "every sutler, cook and camp follower who could write" must have been published during the centennial. Meanwhile, every Civil War battle was refought by centennial writers in a stream of "be-hind-every-tree" studies that informed the reader where every regiment cooked breakfast before the battle of Gettysburg.

This is not to say that some southern authors of that period did not make significant contributions to Civil War historical writing. There were works of high quality, such as Frank Vandiver's biography of Jackson and a general war history, Bell I. Wiley's work in the social impact of the struggle, and Shelby Foote's three-volume epic of the war. Yet even most of the best writing was confined in scope—biography, command and strategic studies, and social history. Except for Shelby Foote's massive trilogy and Frank Vandiver's *Their Tattered Flags*—both completed well after the end of the centennial—there were few efforts by southerners to write the great Confederate iliad, to focus upon the war's tragedy in its entirety.

All of this is to suggest that, despite enthusiasm accompanying the centennial, southern people displayed only a surface interest in the war itself. Confederate Memorial Day has become almost an anachronism in a Dixie society that hustles to build another Atlanta Hyatt-Regency, woo Yankee dollars with Disneyworld and King's Dominion, or obtain more franchises for fast-food establishments. Robert E. Lee's birthday goes unnoticed in much of a region where once schoolteachers were provided manuals giving instructions for proper observance of the holy day. In 1977 about 200,000 people made the pilgrimage to Fort Sumter where the war began, but meanwhile some 100 miles up the South Carolina coast, 4.7 million people journeyed to the sun and sand empire at Myrtle Beach. That same year 138,000 visitors went to Stone's River battlefield, site of one of the Civil War's fiercest engagements; while, thirty miles away, 2 million people were enjoying the garish country-music-theme park at Opryland, U.S.A. It is no surprise that a 1979 poll conducted among a class of students at a large southern university revealed that out of 100 students questioned— almost all natives of the region—75 percent had never heard of the great Confederate hero, General Nathan Bedford Forrest.

Viewers of the national television media during the civil rights disorders of the fifties and sixties might disagree with the suggestion that the Civil War no longer touches southern lives as it once did. An iconography of Confederate symbolism ran through the massive resistance to desegregation in the wake of *Brown* v. *Board of Education of Topeka*. White citizens' councils, the Klan, college students, angry parents—all exhibited the icons. Confederate flags were displayed at prosegregation demonstrations and from college dormitory windows. "Dixie" was sung by street mobs and by well-dressed crowds at lily-white southern football contests, and bumper plates bearing crossed Rebel flags or "Forget Hell" slogans found a healthy market.

In 1979 Bill Sloat in *The South Magazine,* a business organ, interviewed Fred Skillern, president of Dixie Souvenirs, Inc., of Tennessee. Skillern's wholesale company sold tourist items to about one thousand stores in nine southern states. Skillern commented that "When there were racial problems there was a marked increase in the sale of Confederate flags. It would become a superhot item." According to Sloat, the proprietor reported "he could tell towns where federal authorities were forcing school desegregation by watching flag shipments from his factory."

Much of the use of this symbolism waned by the 1970s. Massive resistance to segregation ended, and the white citizens' councils and the Ku Klux Klan were disdained even by many of their southern kinsmen. After passage of the 1965 Civil Rights Act, which dealt chiefly with voting rights, the impact of black people in local politics changed markedly. By 1970, 3.3 million southern blacks had registered to vote, a figure that equaled two-thirds of all those of voting age. There was also the pressure from civil rights groups coupled with the acceptance of black athletes in southern high school and college programs. "Dixie" began to disappear from the repertoire of school marching bands, as did the waving of Confederate flags to celebrate a touchdown scored by a black football star. As Fred Skillern noted, "Rebel-type items aren't as popular as they used to be. . . . I closed my factory where I made them here and buy them now from a place in New Jersey." But Rebel flag bumper plates remain good sellers, Skillern observed, "always up there number two or three in sales." They are icons, just as are the beach towels bearing a Rebel flag, manufactured in Taiwan, the Japanese-produced cigarette lighters that play "Dixie," and the Old South balls at Kappa Alpha fraternity.

Marshall Fishwick observed in *Icons of America* that such physical objects are really modes of expression. Icons are, in effect, synthesizing agents that represent deeply felt inner passions of love, loyalty, or hatred. The display of Confederate artifacts in recent times—whether Confederate flags waving in 1956 when Autherine Lucy enrolled at the University of Alabama or Rebel flag decals on rural southern pickup trucks in the 1970s—probably has little direct connection with the Civil War itself. The odds are good that the individuals displaying the icons never read a biography of Robert E. Lee, or could not identify Perryville, Arkansas Post, or Brandy Station. Instead, the Confederate flag becomes a synthesizer, a physical object to display inner feelings of dislike of authority, alienation from the American experience, racial attitudes, or some other element of southern separatism.

The point is that the memory of defeat—the essence of the Lost Cause—remains central to the white southern mind. The failure of modern Dixie fiction, art, or music to be concerned directly with the Confederacy has little to do with the impact of the Confederate experience upon the modern South. Nor should one be misled to assume that the superficial display of Confederate icons on automobile windows or at football contests is indicative of a lack in the southerner's perception about the real meaning of the Civil War.

The *memory* of the war—not the conflict itself— has always been the focus of the Lost Cause mentality. This is, in effect, the meaning of the phrase itself. The Lost Cause has never been a celebration of the Confederacy, but a monument to defeat. Even in the years immediately after Appomattox, that first angry generation of southern writers—the original Lost Cause artists—focused not upon battles won, but on a war lost. Certainly the postwar magazines, such as the *Southern Historical Society Papers* and *The Land We Love*, printed articles on a broad range of topics, but the chroniclers of the original Inner Lost Cause, such as Jubal Early, John William Jones, Daniel Harvey Hill were not preoccupied with writing traditional battle accounts. The focus was upon what Bernard DeVoto described later as the "Everlasting If"—the metahistorical might-have-been situations where Rebel defeat might have been averted. Many articles concerned the countless disputes over the loss at Gettysburg, the question of the "Lost Order" in the Antietam campaign, the conflict over General P. G. T. Beauregard's command at Shiloh, and other issues where they assumed the Confederacy's fate hung in the balance. Too often, members of this first generation have been depicted as visionaries intoxicated by one last great toast to the chivalric epic. The result of the war—the absolute sense of loss—was the issue that both intrigued and troubled the former Confederates.

This same concern with *loss* and not the war's military history itself also characterized the efforts of the National Lost Cause authors later in the nineteenth century. Unfortunately the local colorists such as Thomas Nelson Page and Sara Pryor dwelled too much upon the South-as-was, splendid mansions, and a knightly social order.

This second generation of Lost Cause authors was concerned with deeper issues. Sara Rice Pryor, author of the well-received *Reminiscences of Peace and War* (1904) and *My Day: Reminiscences of a Long Life*, illustrates the point well. Here were tales of the Virginia lass of Cedar Grove, who married the future Virginia congressman Roger Pryor, and lived through the whirl of Washington's southern-oriented culture on the eve of the Civil War. Well over a century later, one can be charmed easily by Sara Pryor's almost childlike descriptions of her coming of age amid the hegemony of Virginia aristocracy, lush gardens and social elegance. The ultimate result, however, was tragedy. This, too, is documented by Sara Pryor—the chaos of a crumbling order in Virginia as the flames engulfed Richmond, and the ensuing disruption of individual lives.

Here is the essence of the two-edged sword of the National Lost Cause writers. They viewed the South with ambivalence, as a love-hate matter of the idealized agrarian life and the hopelessness of defeat. In brief, the romance-tragedy approach of the National Lost Cause writers was the pioneer effort in literary expression of the basic paradox of southern life.

Much has been written about the distinct perspective of time and place shared by Dixie authors of the later southern renascence. Lewis P. Simpson in his Lamar Lectures at Mercer University suggested that the renascence generation experienced a "recovery of memory and history" grounded in the awesome sense of witnessing a transition from an agrarian to a modern South. To Simpson, previous nineteenth-century southern letters had been confined to a defense of life as it was, is, or is supposed to be, with little feeling for the dichotomy between the pastoral image and reality.

The argument by Simpson and scores of others that the writers of the renascence era possessed this peculiar dimension in toto would be difficult to refute. Much of the brilliance of the generation of writers between the 1920s and 1940s was their expression of paradox—the southerner as regional entity and American, hedonist and religious fundamentalist, noble and tragic.

But the literary expression of this dualistic Lost Cause had begun with the earlier bevy of writers in the late nineteenth century. Sara Pryor may not have lived in the last great age of the Confederate veteran, as did Faulkner, Thomas Wolfe, and others of the renascence, but she did have the chance to marvel at the first wonders of modern technology such as the electric light, the telephone, and the internal combustion engine.

Of course, Sara Pryor was an emigrant and her vision of time and place was sharpened by the stark differences between past and present. Her literary renown came from books written in New York, not in Virginia. Her husband, Roger Pryor, formerly a fiery Virginia secessionist and then Rebel congressman and general, rose by 1894 to serve on the New York State Supreme Court.

Sara Pryor's experiences had given her an unusual perspective shared by another prominent author of the National Lost Cause. Constance Cary, acclaimed as one of the belles of Richmond during the Civil War, was married in 1868 to Burton Harrison, wartime secretary to President Jefferson Davis. Harrison, too, went to New York after the war and became a highly successful legal counselor for Western Union and other companies. Meanwhile his wife, Constance Cary Harrison, delighted national readers with her famous *Reminiscences Grave and Gay* and several novels of life in the Old South.

Both women wrote in a peculiar context of dual alienation and ambivalence. In part, their frame of reference was shaped by their consciousness of being defeated southerners living in a victorious North, of the contrasts between the genteel agrarian ideals and the sprawl of corporate society.

At the same time, Sara Pryor and Constance Harrison were Confederate expatriates who could view their heritage in a distinct perspective. Their reminiscences may have paid tribute to the giddy social whirls of antebellum Virginia and the wartime aristocracy in Richmond, but they also wrote of the glamour of New York society during the late Victorian era. Sara Pryor was nostalgic about the gardens "abloom with roses, lilies, violets, jonquils," and the "dew-washed fruits of an 'old Virginia' garden," but probably could remember as well the slave quarters, lack of "modern" conveniences, and the ashes of Richmond. The old Virginia was a grand memory, but the New York of the early 1900s symbolized America's future with the bustle of fashionable nouveau riche business moguls, electric streetcars, the Four Hundred, Delmonico's, and the Flat-iron Building. This dualistic sense of alienation—the south-erner versus the American, and the southerner at war with himself—was expressed first in Sara Pryor's generation of Dixie authors. It was the core of their Lost Cause rationale—the love-hate blending of the romantic and tragic Souths.

The Janus imagery of the defeated Confederacy did not di-minish in the twentieth century, but came to full bloom during the years of the southern cultural renascence of the twenties and thirties. The southern renascence perhaps has enjoyed the most attention of any cultural event in Dixie thus far in the twentieth century. Louis Rubin, Jr., Walter Sullivan, Hugh Hol-man, and other experts on southern letters have written much about the literary brilliance of the era of Faulkner, Wolfe, and Welty. Meanwhile George Tindall and John Bradbury, among others, have commented upon the South's broader reestablish-ment of a rich cultural heritage in education, literature, and en-deavors witnessed in the decades between the two world wars.

Sometimes overlooked is the fact that the renascence was the first full-scale presentation of the enduring Lost Cause as-sertion of the dichotomy of the virtuous and the tragic in re-gional life. The absolute core of the Lost Cause is nothing more than an expression of the paradoxes rooted deeply in the south-ern mind. Defeat in the Civil War, with all of the subsequent theological, social, and economic consequences, solidified and reinforced the southern perception of existing within an alter-nate society, in a counterculture that often failed to share that bevy of American myths undergirding popular conceptions of our national experience. Few humans probably have been so af-fected by Hegel's "strife of opposites."

The Lost Cause is in actuality a celebration of the southern paradox, and a recognition of the absolute dichotomy of its her-itage. The South is both regional and American—born in a cul-ture but unable to share in its dreams of success and pretense of innocence. There is the absolute struggle between Calvin and Satan—a paradox of hedonism and religious fundamentalism, sensuality and sexual repression. There is the cult of manners juxtaposed often to crudity, intense reverence for the soil opposed to a chamber-of-commerce type of exploitation. This is the real meaning and importance of the Lost Cause to the modern southern mind. Superficial observations have characterized the slogan as the hallmark of a defunct Confederate epoch where gentle and aged ladies of the United Daughters joined forces with diehard racists, professional southerners, a few canny politicians, and others to create from the imagination a land that never was.

At the heart of the literary richness of the southern expression was the writers' awareness of living in a peculiar dimension of time and place, between the agrarian and industrial Souths. The phrase *backward glance* has been worked exhaustively by postrenascence commentators. Still, its overuse does not alter the facts.

Consider that when the Fugitives reassembled at Vanderbilt University after the Great War, Allen Tate, John Crowe Ransom, and the others were aware of the death in 1923 of Flora Cooke Stuart. Seventy years earlier, Flora Cooke had been the commandant's daughter and the belle of Fort Riley, Kansas, where she was wooed by the dashing cavalry lieutenant, J. E. B. Stuart. And in 1917, a full dozen years before William Faulkner's *Sartoris* was published, General Simon Bolivar Buckner had died. Thomas Wolfe already was seventeen years old and Robert Penn Warren was twelve when the Kentucky general, who had surrendered Fort Donelson to Ulysses Grant, died on his Green River farm.

One would be hard-pressed to suggest many other bodies of American writers who have ever benefited from such a dimension of time and place. In 1927, the year of Charles Lindbergh, General John McCausland died in the West Virginia mountains.

In 1864, when General Jubal Early's force approached Washington, McCausland's cavalry had swung north into Pennsylvania, had demanded a ransom from Chambersburg's city fathers, and then had burned the town. Even in 1927 an obituary in a national magazine would still describe him as "the 'Hun' of Chambersburg." And in 1918, when observing England's crisis in the Great War, a biographer of Robert E. Lee, Henry Shepherd, could recollect when he listened to the first inaugural address of President Abraham Lincoln.

Douglas Southall Freeman captured this southern concept of linear time, of a past and present intertwined. In various articles and speeches during the renascence years, Freeman recalled that he had known many people who had heard Daniel Webster and Henry Clay debate, and remembered how he had listened as a youth while his grandfather compared the sounds of a Richmond rainstorm to the guns at Fredericksburg. Freeman was of this last southern generation for whom a Confederate veteran was a reality, and in a 1935 address at Columbia University, he could remember the quaver of the Rebel yell from aged throats as Richmond veterans cheered old General John Gordon's appearance in a reunion parade.

For Freeman, writing in the age of economic disaster and the rise of Hitler, all of this had a meaning far beyond nostalgia. In one radio address titled "How a Great Leader Met Adversity," he compared Robert E. Lee's career after Appomattox with the American economic travail of the 1930s. Freeman's analogy was that Lee was noble in defeat and prevailed over the financial hard times; hence an America in the era of soup kitchens and breadlines should heed the message of Robert E. Lee and the entire South—that it was possible for good men to suffer losses and still retain hope.

The dualistic expression of a South at once romantic and tragic underlies the prolific nonfiction writing on the Civil War during this period. For example, Douglas Freeman's four-volume *R. E. Lee* was undoubtedly the best historical work on the war published during the renascence. The biography is a classic restatement of the romance-tragedy image fashioned in the late nineteenth-century by southern authors. Freeman's Lee was the product of an aristocratic system that ennobled order and taught a sense of values. Eventually Lee was entrapped by the very environment that had wrought his nobility, and was fixed between his inbred sense of honor and the slavocracy he disliked.

The ambivalence of Freeman's hero is characteristic of the period's attitude toward the Lost Cause and the entire southern experience. It permeates serious fiction in such novels as Caroline Gordon's *None Shall Look Back*. Fontaine Allard and his family exist in a doomsday world of tragedy; at the same time, the *idea* of a planter aristocracy—the complex web of a code of values—becomes an object that has relevance for the present time. The same dichotomy existed in popular fiction during the renascence. In an essay on Margaret Mitchell's *Gone With the Wind*, Darden Pryor noted that the author's concept of Georgia aristocracy was far different from the Hollywood depiction of a blend of strength and luxury in the planter society. Margaret Mitchell's Georgia was a land of the red-clay new rich, Tara was certainly no grand manor, and the Ashley Wilkeses were effete and almost pathetic. Still, as Pryor noted in his essay, Margaret Mitchell obviously was aware of the paradox of romance and tragedy. Weak though the aristocracy was in her conception, it represented an *ideal* that gained a mythical strength in Clayton County that it had not possessed before the fall of Atlanta. The national response to the southern renascence has been well documented. Eventually, by the 1960s, *Gone With the Wind* had sold almost seven million copies. The success of this one drama has overshadowed the fact that during the renascence years, there was a strong national demand for the Janus image of the South. Stark Young's *So Red the Rose* was a best-selling novel, Shirley Temple and Bill "Bojangles" Robinson charmed millions in *The Littlest Rebel*, and Du Pont's "Cavalcade of America" radio series in 1940 eulogized Robert E. Lee as the epitome of romance and tragedy.

A single issue of the *Saturday Review of Literature* in 1943—when the renascence was still a potent factor—may provide an explanation for the surge of national interest in the southern epic spanning the years from 1861 to 1865. There was, for example, a full-page advertisement for a southern romantic novel by Maritan Simms titled *Beyond Surrender* that promised readers the book spoke of "flesh-and-blood people who faced a problem not unlike the one which confronts us today." There was a notice as well for Willa Cather's *Sapphira and the Slave Girl*, which helped "recreate the Old South," and another for Clare Leighton's *Southern Harvest*, in which the reader not only "feels the South," but shares something deeper. He experiences also "the common quality of man's earth—sustained living." This element of "sustained living" is perhaps the core of the overwhelming national response to southern imagery during the 1930s. Never before had the noble-tragic appeal of the Lost Cause possessed such relevance.

On the surface, the national fascination with the plantation mythology, what Jack Kirby described as the image of the Grand Old South, was pure escapism from the anxieties of economic misery and international turmoil. The popular culture that produced Shirley Temple's *The Littlest Rebel* or read Francis Griswold's *The Tides of Malvern* was part of a larger search for a fantasy of relief akin to interest in the tinsel musical films of Fred Astaire and Ginger Rogers or the radio comedy of Fred Allen's "Town Hall Tonight."

The escapist image of a happy, luxuriant antebellum South permeated American popular culture during the depression years of the 1930s. The nostalgic Old South was stock-in-trade in an entire genre of films offered by Hollywood. In 1935

The Little Colonel and *The Littlest Rebel* reinforced the imagery of a Grand Old Dixie resplendent with Hattie McDaniel as the wise mammy of *The Little Colonel* and Bill Robinson as the Uncle Tomish butler of both films. Stepin Fetchit became a millionaire portraying the stupid, helpless black in films such as *Carolina* and *Steamboat 'Round the Bend*.

Those Americans who stayed home during the thirties and read books instead, were treated to the same cavalier escapism. Stark Young's *Heaven Trees* (1926) had initiated the saga of Mississippi planters, the McGhee-Clay-Bedford amalgam, woven around Heaven Trees Plantation. Young's *So Red the Rose*, a national bestseller and a successful motion picture in the mid-thirties, presented the orthodox image of the romantic South. The protagonist, Duncan Bedford, and his family lived in "a lovely and secret place," and represented the total of the southern code of behavior. Francis Griswold's *The Tides of Malvern* and *A Sea Island Lady* re-created much of this same imagery in the story of the Sheldon family of South Carolina, as Joseph Hergesheimer did for the Sash family in Kentucky.

But the obvious high-water mark of the romantic side of the Lost Cause was the 1939 screen adaptation of *Gone With the Wind*, which by 1971 had earned perhaps over $100 million in film rentals alone. The national phenomenon of *Gone With the Wind* and its cinema success has been told time and again—of David O. Selznick's famous search for an actress to portray Scarlett O'Hara, the glitter of the famous Atlanta premiere, and the immense financial returns of the novel as well as the film.

Certainly *Gone With the Wind* also described Jack Kirby's Grand Old South. The already familiar mosaic of plantation splendor, contented servants, and strong aristocrats dominated the cinema version. Mitchell may have attempted to portray a society of red-clay new-rich southerners, where the male planters were weak and ineffectual, but regardless of her intentions, a quality of nobility remains after the aristocracy is defeated in the Civil War. It is a story of southern endurance seen in other popular southern fiction of the era. In *So Red the Rose, The Tides of Malvern,* and others, the ghost of planter aristocracy gains strength as the *ideal* of order and principle. Here is the real importance of the national interest in the southern heritage during the renascence years. Margaret Mitchell's novel and similar cultural expressions were a restatement of the dualism of the National Lost Cause writers of the late nineteenth century. For example, *Gone With the Wind* contained the same two basic ingredients that characterize the earlier writings of George Cary Eggleston, Sara Pryor, and Thomas Nelson Page. The dualistic Lost Cause remained. Although the antebellum southern life was destroyed by war, the principles instilled by such an environment survived in the resplendent examples of Robert E. Lee and other southerners, even in the wake of the tragic defeat at Appomattox.

This image of southern nobility, of greatness amid despair, appealed to an America of the 1930s. In 1936, when Jesse Jones, head of the Reconstruction Finance Corporation, dedicated the Robert E. Lee statue in Dallas, Texas, he praised the General's principles of the Old South, but Jones centered upon Lee's ability to triumph over adversity after his surrender.

Here again was admiration for that sense of order, at least as an ideal, as found in the aristocratic agrarianism of such fiction writers as Caroline Gordon and Katherine Anne Porter of the renascence. Even the cynicism wrought by the depression had failed to eradicate totally that concern for the old agrarian verities. Bruce Barton's 1920s characterization of a self-made Jesus in a gray flannel suit, in books such as *The Man Nobody Knows* still possessed impact, as did the public imagery of rugged individualistic hero ideals such as "Babe" Ruth and the "Lone Eagle." The belief in stability and order remained vital to the culture of the thirties despite the disillusionment after the collapse of Wall Street. Clark Gable and Claudette Colbert idealized the concept of romantic love in *It Happened One Night*, and the basic ideals of the Ringo Kid remained important in John Ford's metaphor of agrarian-urban conflict in the classic western cinema *Stagecoach*.

Equally important is the fact that during the depression era, the nation could identify more than ever before with the Lost Cause imagery of the tragic hero. A generation of Americans had marched off to the Great War believing that it would ensure peace and preserve a way of life. Yet by 1936 the nation had witnessed the rise of fascism in Europe and the invasion of mainland China by Japan.

Moreover, a people reared on the optimistic writings of Horatio Alger, Jr., and Harold Bell Wright—who preached of the tie between morality and success—was now disillusioned. Millions had accepted the Calvinistic tenet that moral uprightness wrought material reward, that the nation was a land of irrevocable promise. But the American faith in progress had dissipated during the depression years, as it had for the South in the aftermath of 1865. Millions in the 1930s could now question whether the old doctrine of preordained American victory was valid, and begin to doubt the tales of success that had been written by Edward Bok and others.

Never before had the entire nation been so close to the southern experience. On one hand, there was an expression of skepticism that forced a new examination of the concept of inevitable American progress and success. It was apparent in the reaction to the report of Senator Gerald Nye's Senate committee that suggested the Great War had been produced by a connivance of munitions manufacturers and international financiers; in Walter Mill's *The Road to War* which challenged the American psyche of inevitability and suggested that the path to the First World War was a gigantic blunder; and in the hollow stares of the sharecroppers in Erskine Caldwell's and Margaret Bourke-White's *You Have Seen Their Faces*.

Never before had the entire nation come so close to empathy with that southern sense of piety that viewed life as a classical tragedy—the unbending human endeavor struggling with impossible odds, with knowledge of man's limitations with an order of coexistent good and evil. Dixie authors could still express it with more force. One of the best treatments was an obscure article by Sara Hardt in a 1930 issue of the *American Mercury*. She had gone back home to attend a cemetery observance of Confederate Memorial Day in an Alabama community. At first she felt repelled by the acrid scent of flowers wilting in the "long lavender shadows" on the hillside. But then the writer was gripped by a sense of melancholy when she realized that by living so close "to these dead and dying things" she could never get away completely. Her awareness of being trapped by the past led her to embrace "a philosophy of futility . . . that is the curse of all Southerners." The point is that the traditional American faith in inevitable change and progress had been weakened by events of the thirties, and the southern concept of the inevitable presence of evil seemed more valid. Many Americans simply no longer trusted their history, and they feared their future.

No era of history received more jaundiced reappraisal than did the Civil War. The war's causes came under scrutiny by an impressive array of revisionist historians, led by Professor James Randall of the University of Illinois. Randall lashed out at those who viewed the Civil War as a romantic scenario and who labeled it a senseless effort that produced typhus, venereal disease and other agonies, and asserted that "Lincoln's generation stumbled into a ghastly war." Meanwhile Professor Avery Craven in *The Repressible Conflict* belittled the notion that the war was the result of grandiose social forces enwrapped in principles of inevitable national progress, and asserted that the nation simply went mad and tumbled into the catastrophe. Then Professor Charles Ramsdell, the third member of the triumvirate of Civil War revisionists, produced a famous article on "Lincoln and Fort Sumter" which argued that the American president manipulated the nation into war in order to save the Republican party and his own political fortunes.

Ramsdell's Lincoln stressed the human factor—the power of the individual to alter history. A depression generation that suspected industrial moguls of manipulating the tragedy of the First World War and Wall Street magnates of causing the crash of 1929 could believe that great cataclysm could be influenced by human machinations. Such a view was essentially the heart of the Lost Cause argument that had been advanced by southern local colorists in the late nineteenth century and restated by authors of the renascence. Bold men with public images larger than life could have altered the war's fortunes in an instant, but they experienced tragic failure.

One is drawn again to Bernard DeVoto's essay that practically admitted the triumph of this mentality in the war fiction of the 1930s. DeVoto's descriptions of "The Everlasting If" and "a great perhaps" as dominating the contemporary writing on the Civil War was nothing more than an expression of the southern concept of time and place, and the romance-tragedy imagery of the Lost Cause.

The concept of the tragic hero suspended between past and present may have been the primary southern expression, but temporarily during the thirties became a theme used by other Americans who now shared a sense of abject failure. DeVoto bore down upon the theme in a *Harper's* essay on Gettysburg, in which he suggested that "the pattern of Western Civilization" rested upon the deeds committed there by men within a few hours. The revisionists such as James Randall and Avery Craven centered their argument of the Repressible Conflict upon the prime human ability to save or destroy. Winston Churchill's "If Lee Had Not Won the Battle of Gettysburg" appeared in a 1930 issue of *Scribner's*; the editor explained that

Churchill was writing about the different society that would have existed "merely if the South had won a single battle." Later, in 1942, Henry Steele Commager, in an article in *Scholastic* magazine, summarized over a decade of such revisionist thought. Commager said that southern defeat was not inevitable. To assume that "would make those responsible for secession and war to be reckless fools." Instead, Commager observed, the South had from the outset, "an excellent chance to achieve independence" that did not fade until the last months of the conflict.

American victory in the Second World War was a prelude to over two decades of changing opinions regarding the image of the Confederate South. The outcome of the war and the rise of the nuclear age negated the pessimistic, isolationist views of the thirties that had found the Confederate symbolism of courage amid defeat so attractive. The new nationalism evident in the postwar generation was centered upon more immediate concerns, such as the hydrogen bomb, the Cold War, and the rise of Middle America suburbia of the fifties.

For the two decades following 1950, the progress of America's internal growth in industry, urbanization, and transportation seemed to accelerate the distance between national empathy and the Lost Cause. By the end of the sixties, massive changes had so affected the South that observers questioned whether a separate regional culture still existed.

This Americanization of the South has been a persistent reality since the Second World War. Those who decry the demise of the Lost Cause have pointed to numerous factors that, at first glance, appear difficult to refute. There has been an erosion of "traditional" attitudes and practices of segregation and one-party political rule. Simultaneously, the influx of industry, the television medium, and interstate highway transportation apparently has broken down many vestiges of regionalism. Consumers are in line with national trends, southern cities boast professional teams that compete in national leagues, and the fabric of Dixie's public and private architecture exhibits qualities of the standardization of American life.

At the same time, however, it could be argued that a southern regionalism still exists within the form of a *gemeinschaft*, a persistent folk culture. Howard Odum observed in 1947 that the way of the South was the "culture of the folk." Sociologist Clifford Geertz has defined a culture as a myriad of historical meanings. These are transformed from generation to generation by powerful symbols, which not only perpetuate a legacy of ideals, but shape contemporary attitudes as well.

The southern *Gemeinschaft* of the middle and late twentieth century may well be grounded in three important elements. First, there is the presence of a different historical tradition, as C. Vann Woodward observed in *The Burden of Southern History*. Woodward commented upon the South's lack of sharing in basic American myths of success and innocence. In his essay "The Search for Southern Identity," he noted the leveling qualities of the cultural Americanization of the South, but postulated that the regional identity might be kept alive by consciousness of this heritage of *difference*.

The southern culture of the folk possibly might also be sustained by an awareness that others regard Dixie as different. Sociologist Lewis Killian's study *White Southerners* pronounced them a defined minority in American society, for many reasons. One reason was the presence of a "minority psychology," in which white southerners were aware not only of Woodward's realities of alienation from the American dream, but believed as well that nonsoutherners viewed them as a collective minority.

There is a third element in this suggestion of a separate folk culture that involves neither Tate's "backward glance" nor Killian's regional defensiveness. It is perhaps the most difficult to define because of the intangible nature, the alchemy, of modern southern values and traditions. Charles Roland in his study of modern Dixie, *The Improbable Era*, described the steady nationalization of regional culture, but reinforced the paradox of a southern continuity of attitude. Roland suggested that, amid the influx of American sameness below the Potomac, a quality of difference remained. The differences, he observed, are grounded in "subtle inner distinctions." These distinctions have been noted by many observers of the modern South's folk culture. Although they have approached the matter from different perspectives, the consensus remains that a separate quality of myth, tradition, and values characterizes the South despite the compelling forces of modernization. Louis D. Rubin, Jr., in his essay "Second Thoughts on the Old Gray Mare," continued his long, splendid debate with Vanderbilt critic and writer Walter Sullivan on the status of regional literature. Professor Sullivan's contention was that the inspiration of the writers of the southern renascence came from participation in a society that witnessed the last days of the moral order of the Old South in terms of religion, race, and otherwise. Rubin's suggestion was that the South endured despite gnosticism and Atlanta's Omni, and existed within a framework of attitudes derived from history and memory.

Rubin never established the absolutes of this folk culture, but spoke of the intangibles. Alfred Hero's *The Southerner and World Affairs* utilized statistical data to document a continuing parochial view of affairs outside of the South. The foremost expert on southern protestantism, Samuel Hill, spoke of the enduring medley of traditions and values—often with religious overtones—that characterized the region.

Regional attitudes—particularly those involving the intangibles of the mercurial southern nature—are difficult to document and consequently lay themselves prone to frequent speculation. Still, John Shelton Reed's study, *The Enduring South: Subcultural Persistence in Mass Society*, appears to reinforce the existence of this third facet of the totality of a separate southern folk culture. Reed's examination, based upon data obtained from sources such as the Roper Public Opinion Research Center, the Louis Harris Political Data Center, and other sources, suggests that "a vigorous regional subculture" remains in a Dixie immersed in the American context of mass society. Sociologist Reed's findings note three particular areas of distinction in attitudes and beliefs below the Potomac, and it is no accident that all are related to the imagery of the Lost Cause. First, continuing concern with fundamentalist religious tenets gives validity to H. L. Mencken's scoffing that Dixie was "the last great bulwark of Christianity" and the "defender of the ark." Polls in the early 1960s revealed that 75 percent of southern Protestants interviewed still claimed membership in the triumvirate of those evangelical faiths that flourished after Appomattox—Southern Baptist, Methodist, and Presbyterian; in non-South areas, only 41 percent expressed such leanings. Meanwhile, the southern belief in an anthropomorphic Satan, as a member of the Trinity with God and man, remained strong. A 1957 poll of Protestants on the question of belief in Satan revealed that 86 percent of Dixie people believed, while only 52 percent of nonsoutherners accepted the reality of Lucifer.

Reed's data revealed also a continuing southern difference of attitude toward the use of force to settle differences—the proverbial "Smith and Wesson Line." For example, one 1968 poll indicated that 52 percent of southerners interviewed admitted possessing firearms in their homes, as opposed to 27 percent in non-South regions.

Finally, Reed examined the distinct southern attachment to family and community. The resulting evidence substantiated that at least the *attitude*, if not the reality of southern localism remained strong in a transient America where physical or emotional bonds with time and place have been weakened by improved transportation, the mass media, and opportunities for economic betterment. For example, in a 1950 poll, 55 percent of those southerners questioned as to where they would move if forced to leave their present state chose another Dixie region; meanwhile only 11 percent of people in the middle Atlantic region elected to remain in their area.

Regardless of the variables present in Reed's statistics—which he freely admits—the study presented a strong case for the persistence of regional attitudes within a mass American culture. C. Vann Woodward's reminder of the great southern burden of memory, Lewis Killian's observations on Dixie awareness of existence as a counterculture, and Reed's documentation of strong divergence in some basic opinions all give strength to Louis Rubin's observation that the "Old Gray Mare" of Dixie attitudes persists amid a whirl of change.

The South retains a folk culture heavily endowed with memory and legend, and this is the essence of the Lost Cause. The meaning of the Lost Cause to modern southerners involves no maudlin recall of wisteria, banjos, and Stephen Foster melodies. Nor does the definition of the phrase relate to a precise knowledge of the Confederacy or a particular interest in the exploits of the Rebel army beyond the occasional display of icons such as flags.

The essence of the modern Lost Cause is not the South of 1861, but the Confederacy of 1865. It is an awareness of defeat, alienation from the national experience, and a sense of separatism from American ideals. It is not the totality of southern folk culture, but remains a strong central element. John Shelton Reed's summation of the persistence of a Dixie subculture amid national change centered upon regional attitudes toward violence, religion, and localism. All three have been integral parts of the Lost Cause mythology since Appomattox. In fact, they are embedded in the Dixie sense of memory and history to a degree that probably no Americanization of the South could erase totally.

There is a second reason why the Lost Cause has not perished.

Very simply, the remainder of the nation would not allow it. Marshall Frady, commenting in a 1975 issue of *Newsweek*, recalled the professor at an Iowa university who badgered a southern student to explain why Dixie people cherish being apart from the remainder of the United States. Frady observed that part of the reason was "the rest of the country has always been so eager to collaborate in the mystique," and that the South has given the American fancy "a kind of running domestic theater of the dreamy and fantastic."

Three potential uses of the Lost Cause mythology may have been present in the modern America outside of Dixie. First, the South old and new serves as a *contrast*, to Middle American values. The media portrayals of the South presented in the fifties and sixties were reinforcements of the American self-image of innocence and fairness. Jack Kirby, in *Media-Made Dixie*, observed how the continual reshaping of the Dixie image by the national media—especially in the genre of entertainment—perhaps told more about America's moods than it did about Dixie. For example, in the Eisenhower years of Middle American stability amid the backwash of pride in victory in the Second World War, the nation had lost much of the depression era's empathy with the tragic-hero southern image. An American middle class could lounge in recreation rooms and observe via television the ugly opening scenes of massive resistance to desegregation at Clinton, Tennessee, and Little Rock, Arkansas in the late fifties. Soon after came the sordid James Meredith incident at the University of Mississippi, the church bombing in Birmingham, the murders in Philadelphia, Mississippi, the assassination of Dr. Martin Luther King, Jr.

From the self-confident Eisenhower years until the early 1970s, Hollywood's portrayal of the South old and new reinforced the Middle American self-image of righteousness, fairness, and stability. The modern South displayed in dozens of cinema offerings such as *Cat on a Hot Tin Roof, God's Little*

Acre, The Long Hot Summer, The Defiant Ones, Sweet Bird of Youth, Inherit the Wind, and many others was an alchemy of neurotic aristocrats, sexual degeneracy, violence, intolerance, and psychopathic behavior. The imagery of the Old South had departed from the romance of *Gone With the Wind* or *Song of the South.*

By the early 1970s, the American use of the Lost Cause imagery took other approaches. A peculiar mixture of conservatism, escapism, and public cynicism was the legacy of the disaster in Vietnam, the disclosures of Watergate, disgust with the counterculture of the 1960s, busing controversies in northern cities, and political and racial unrest and rioting in nonsouthern communities.

Media-Made Dixie chronicled a huge list of evidences that, in the national media, the South had again become respectable. The television offering "The Waltons," based on Earl Hamner, Jr.'s boyhood in the depression-ridden Virginia Blue Ridge Mountains, was a huge success—boasting forty million viewers each week by 1973. The image of the law-and-order South in the film *Walking Tall* appealed to an America weary of riots and to a public skeptical that problems could be resolved through normal political processes. Meanwhile the goatee and stringed tie of the Kentucky Colonel Sanders and the bumbling but lovable southern sheriff in advertisements of the Chrysler Corporation became familiar objects. So, too, did North Carolina's Senator Sam Ervin, during the Senate Watergate hearings.

The ultimate of the new southern respectability came in 1976, when a born-again Southern Baptist peanut farmer, Jimmy Carter, became president of the United States. Big-city reporters and prophets of the electronic media hastened to Confederate south Georgia to soak up the local atmosphere of kudzu, red clay, and fried-everything hospitality. Until his personal problems sullied the image, the President's brother, Billy, enjoyed a stint as the professional southern good ol' boy, replete with the imagery of beer drinking, rural gasoline stations, and pickup trucks.

Yet any serious analysis of the caricature of the modern folk imagery of the Dixie good ol' boy uncovers a complex mosaic of attitudes. The real importance of the good ol' boy—depicted by numerous Hollywood films in the 1970s—was that he represented southern ambivalence. He is the Lost Cause reincarnate—a paradoxical symbol of those eternal southern opposites, such as a longing for order and a penchant for evasion of the law, deeply embedded religious fundamentalism and hedonistic behavior, Dixie braggadocio, and insecurity.

The America of the mid-seventies could identify with such paradoxes, as the nation in the years of the southern renascence was attracted to the romance-tragedy imagery of the Lost Cause. On one hand, a nation weary with street turmoil and tales of political corruption could appreciate Earl Hamner's explanation that his television family, "The Waltons," was interested in "reaffirming such old-fashioned virtues as self-reliance, thrift, independence, freedom, love of God." Yet the cynicism, with the formal political process that exploded in radical displays of the sixties was felt even by conservatives after the Watergate disclosures. Only the motives were different. Americans of the seventies flocked by the millions to view the original film *Walking Tall* (which earned $35 million in two years) and two sequels.

Both "The Waltons" and the violent tale of the career of Tennessee sheriff Buford Pusser were not really films about the South. They were American metaphors. "The Waltons" used a southern setting to reaffirm a set of agrarian values that provided comfort in the early 1970s. *Walking Tall* was a metaphor of an American desire for return to law and order intermingled with a contrasting disdain for the formal legal process. Sheriff Pusser embodied the image of a vigilante, whose use of violence, power, and extra-legal means wrought order and reinforced tranquillity in McNairy County, Tennessee.

Here is a second reason the nation probably will not allow the Lost Cause to rest in peace. The South as metaphor possesses a distinct appeal to the outside world. After all, southerners are Americans, however exaggerated their temper may be to the non-Dixie observer. A strong case could be offered that at least in the realm of recent national entertainment media, Americans have perceived extremes in Dixie people that serve as an allegory of their own existence.

The South as metaphor was observed, for example, in the highly successful television series, "The Andy Griffith Show." Supposedly the series was a light-hearted story of the life of a sheriff in a small North Carolina community. Actually little southern symbolism was apparent. Instead, the humor and pathos exhibited by the display of town characters was a story of Crossroads, U.S.A. with its medley of goodness, hypocrisy, and nostalgia. The motion picture version of James Dickey's novel *Deliverance* was a complex metaphor of the clash between Middle American urbanization and raw, primitive culture. Robert Altman's celebrated *Nashville* was based upon the paradoxes of the folkish-religious atmosphere of Nashville and the cynical rhinestone world of country music. Yet Altman considered the film to be an allegory of modern America, in which imagination (or faith) fights an endless battle with pragmatism (or cynicism) over the nature of reality.

More important, the image of the South as an alternate society has intrigued Americans in the twentieth century. Walter Prescott Webb's *The Great Frontier* spoke of how an industrial, urban society, burdened with an imbalanced population-land ratio, could no longer view the vanished frontier as even an emotional safety valve. In recent times, the image of Dixie in the nonsouthern mind has provided the nation with the promise of an alternative society.

The modern American attitude toward the Lost Cause image has on occasion fluctuated sharply between admiration and violent disapproval. Depending upon the prevailing national mood, there has been in particular a constant struggle between the South as alternate and the South as contrast. The American of the 1930s was disillusioned by economic disaster and world turmoil, and doubted the old verities of inevitable progress. The alternate image of the Lost Cause South as an example of noble behavior amid defeat possessed a strong appeal. Conversely, the American of the 1950s, flush with a new sense of victory, preferred the symbolism of the South as contrast— a degenerate, intolerant society juxtaposed against national innocence.

By the early 1970s, a changed national mood again viewed the South as an alternate society with considerable appeal. This new attractiveness of the Dixie mystique was apparent in three cultural phenomena. All three are related to the endurance of the Lost Cause in the southern memory.

First, a new southern protestantization of America has occurred during the past two decades. It is evident in the huge growth of southern evangelical bodies in the United States. Billy Graham's Southern Baptist crusade was a Dixie-based organization in the fifties; Graham is now an international figure, almost a Protestant pope whose entree to American society ranges from conferences at the White House to massive crusades in northern urban areas. Meanwhile the Southern Baptist faith has grown tremendously across the United States. Membership climbed from 3.6 million in 1950 to 11.6 million by 1970. The Methodist Episcopal, Presbyterian, Pentecostal, and other faiths that are products of the Lost Cause mentality in late nineteenth-century Dixie have grown as well.

This is part of a larger cultural explosion of evangelical Christianity in the America of the post-Watergate and Vietnam era. There has been a massive surge of Christians who claim to have been born again—to have experienced some turning point where their lives were marked by new commitment to Jesus Christ. A 1976 Gallup Poll revealed that 34 percent of Americans interviewed—representing nearly fifty million American adults—lay claim to such an experience. In fact, nearly one-half (48 percent) of Protestants interviewed believed they had had a spiritual reconversion.

The born-again movement, in turn, is part of a larger tide of an evangelical crusade that swept through the United States in the 1970s. *Time* magazine reported in 1977 that the new evangelical crusade—involving 45.5 million Americans, was "once patronized as Southern rural and redneck." The new evangelism has cut across all lines of race, social status, and religion. It represents a membership that ranges from faith healers to nearly a million born-again Roman Catholics, from fundamentalist churchmen to a vast charismatic practice of divine "gifts" such as healing and speaking in tongues that is grounded in southern Pentecostal religion.

A multimillion dollar television and radio network preaches a new conservative faith, grounded in southern fundamentalism. A 1980 article in *American Film* magazine noted the presence of 1,400 radio stations, thirty-eight television stations and sixty-six cable systems which specialize in religious broadcasting. Almost all of the moguls of this new media evangelism broadcast from Dixie. Southern media crusaders such as Pat Robertson, Jim Bakker, and Oral Roberts operate with yearly broadcast budgets of $50 million and more. Meanwhile, in the 1980 presidential election campaign, all three major candidates—Jimmy Carter, Ronald Reagan, and John Anderson—attested to having had a born-again experience.

Much of this new wave of revivalism is rooted in a southern-based faith that flourished and provided succor in post–Civil War Dixie. The types of modern evangelism appear to vary greatly. Yet many of the emphatic features are ones familiar to students of the southern mind. Examine the soul-searching of generations of former Confederates, and the theological similarities with many born-again Americans of the late twentieth century are very real. There is the same stress on individual salvation, Jesus as one's personal savior, and God's Divine Providence as an ever-constant companion. At the same time, there is in both an admission of the presence of evil in one's life, coupled with a sense of other-worldness that foresees no ultimate perfection on earth. Man is a sinner in need of a salvation that ensures a better world. This theology provided comfort for two societies enmeshed in crisis and an awareness of defeat, one of Jubal Early and P. G. T. Beauregard, the other of Jimmy Carter and Charles Colson.

Equally striking is the presence of the South as alternative, which appeared strongly in the national popular culture of the 1970s. A large genre of films such as *Walking Tall*, *Smokey and the Bandit*, and *Every Which Way But Loose* grossed enormous profits. Such films were portrayals of that mystique of Dixie individualism encompassed in the image of the good ol' boy. The cinema offerings were a mixture of violence, law-and-order, fast automobiles, and sex. The stress was upon the protagonist who, while fighting evil, exhibited human weaknesses as well. Good was achieved by vigilante tactics, by operating slightly outside of the confining aspects of the law. To a nation emerging from civil turmoil and disillusionment with its political leaders, the southern image was a welcome change.

Far more important was the phenomenal rise of American interest in country music during the sixties and seventies. Only recently have historians examined this native American music with seriousness. Scholars such as Professor William Malone, in *Country Music U.S.A.* and Professor Charles Wolfe in *Tennessee Strings* have pioneered in a scholarly approach to the topic.

Until the 1960s country music was still regarded as something designed for rural and blue-collar social groups, particularly southerners. In fact, when the country music industry first took root in Nashville, Tennessee, during the 1940s, even local white-collar southerners regarded it with scorn. On one occasion during the forties, the governor of Tennessee refused to appear at a public function honoring country music because he feared that it would stamp Nashville with the image of being the world's "hillbilly capital."

Now country music is a billion-dollar industry in Nashville, which ranks as one of the nation's leading recording centers. The musicians once stylized as "hillbillies" sit on the boards of directors of banks, and even national politicians—such as Jimmy Carter and Richard Nixon—have curried their favor. Meanwhile the entire nation has become involved in country music. Nashville singers frequently are hosts to their own network television specials, several thousand American radio stations play the music, and Nashville continues its vast output to the outside world. The city boasts over two hundred music publishers, fifty recording studios, and a population of several thousand performers, songwriters, studio musicians, and other workers in the burgeoning industry.

One irony of country music is that it has never been involved directly with the theme of the Civil War. Like other varieties of the rich southern musical tradition—blues, rhythm and blues, and others—country music has had little to say directly about the Civil War. A serious student of this music would be hard pressed to uncover more than a very few songs that speak of the Confederacy. One that did was a 1960s recording by folksinger Joan Baez titled "The Night They Drove Old Dixie Down," a stream-of-consciousness ballad about the collapse of Confederate resistance in Virginia during the last weeks of the Civil War. It is important that Joan Baez's lament was concerned with the fall of the Confederacy. Country music may say little directly about the Civil War, but is grounded squarely in the absolute of southern defeat. A strong case could be made that for the average southerner, who reads little or nothing by Allen Tate, William Faulkner, or Robert Penn Warren, country music is the great modern expression of the Lost Cause mentality.

The core of this music is continual striving amid perpetual disappointment—that is at the heart of the Lost Cause. Country music first gained strength among southerners in the 1940s, when they faced the massive changes wrought by the Second World War and its aftermath. The music expressed for many people what they were unable to verbalize for themselves. It spoke of the strains placed on traditional Dixie family ties by the Selective Service and the huge migration of southerners to industrial communities outside of their sense of community. The sense of time and place had been disrupted by the draft, and by the demand for workers in the expanding petrochemical industry of the Gulf Coast, aircraft factories in California, and war production plants in the Midwest.

From this nucleus, the modern genre of country music enlarged into a general expression of many of the ideas of the Lost Cause. The surface themes were expressed in lyrics often crude but never lacking in realism. The songs were of marital strains, adultery, guilt, alcoholism, broken homes, loneliness, and hard financial times. These primary themes were mirrors of an entire southern paradox of opposites. In the music, women became either docile, domestic nonentities or passionate, immoral temptresses. Male superiority is asserted with an air of bravado tempered by absolute insecurity. Traditional southern religion is heralded amid guilt-ridden confessions of hedonistic behavior. A stubborn, optimistic determination to surmount difficulties in marriage, financial affairs, or personal behavior is tempered by a clear-cut confession of mortality.

It is also a music of the paradoxes of the Lost Cause. There is the presence of defeat, counteracted by a continual human striving which speaks of the themes of a classical tragedy. There is the Christian-classical realization of the constant presence of good and evil, and success and failure. Also, the music is underscored with the dichotomies of that constant sense of alienation basic to country music. Man is good but bad, southern yet American, successful yet somehow a failure. It is a music far more noble than the public images of the rhinestone-clad singers from the red-clay farms who have conveyed it to the American public. The public image of Nashville country singers is not one of either trust or appeal. The mental picture is one of uneducated folk from humble beginnings who flaunt stardom by displaying garish mansions and expensive automobiles, and of singers who display at once a tradition of fundamental religion and a personal life-style that squarely contradicts their pietistic roots.

Yet the paradoxes in their lives are only aberrations of the opposites in the broader southern mind, and in the Lost Cause mentality as well. The classic example of this is, of course, Elvis Presley. His influence in shaping—or representing—vast changes in national attitudes in the 1950s and 1960s has been discussed at length by serious observers of American popular culture and its music. Equally well known is the saga of his contradictory image—the modest boy from a poor, illiterate background who reaped millions and flaunted his success in a garish manner and the devoted son and deeply religious Pentecostal lad whose life ended in a tragic epic of bizarre conduct.

Despite these contradictions, the South responded in 1977 to Elvis Presley's death with an outpouring of grief unmatched since the 1870 funeral of Robert E. Lee. After all, Elvis Presley in life and death personified the paradoxes in all southerners. The tales of his drug abuse were counteracted by the undeniable reality of devotion to his mother. Presley's flamboyant arrogance and display of wealth were countered by his image of public humility. His reputation for success and wealth was contradicted by media reports of incessant personal problems and insecurities. More important, his national image of glitter and power was set against the undeniables of his deep roots in southern folkways. Elvis Presley was one of his own Dixie people, but he represented something far beyond the confines of Tupelo, Mississippi, as well. He was the American dream of success but was the southern image of man's awareness of his mortality.

He has been in the years since the southern renascence, the most obvious public symbol of the Lost Cause. As mentioned, few songs that arose from the genre of country music have been concerned directly with the Civil War. Elvis Presley popularized one of the few. This medley styled the "American Trilogy," which contained excerpts from "Dixie," the gentle slave melody of resignation "All My Trials," and the triumphant "Battle Hymn of the Republic." It is a melody that unites the expressions of one's awareness of being at once southern and American, hopeful and limited in aspirations, good and evil. It is the message of the enduring Lost Cause.

NOTE ON SOURCES

The literature of the Lost Cause is, on one hand, voluminous, since the topic embraces all of southern history and literature after the Civil War. Yet there are few actual studies of the development of the Lost Cause mentality itself. Rollin Osterweis' *The Myth of the Lost Cause, 1865–1900* (Hamden, Conn.: Anchor Books, 1973) provides some useful data on the movement but is very incomplete. William White's *The Confederate Veteran* (Tuscaloosa: University of Alabama Press, 1962) is a well-researched account of some aspects of postwar organizational activities, such as the United Confederate Veterans. Far more thoughtful is Richard Weaver's *The Southern Tradition at Bay: A History of Post-Bellum Thought,* edited by George Core and M. E. Bradford (New Rochelle, N.Y.: Arlington House, 1968). See also Paul Buck, *The Road to Reunion, 1865–1900* (Boston: Little, Brown, 1937).

Far more abundant is material on the relationship between southern literature and the Lost Cause mentality. Louis D. Rubin, Jr., has contributed much to the concept of the endurance of the southern memory. One is advised to consult *The Faraway Country: Writers of the Modern South* (Seattle: University of Washington Press, 1963); *William Elliott Shoots a Bear: Essays on the Southern Literary Imagination* (Baton Rouge: Louisiana State University Press, 1975); *The Writer in the South: Studies in a Literary Community* (Athens: University of Georgia Press, 1972); with Robert D. Jacobs, *South: Modern Southern Literature in Its Cultural Setting* (New York: Doubleday, 1961); with Robert D. Jacobs, *Southern Renascence: The Literature of the Modern South* (Baltimore, Md.: Johns Hopkins University Press, 1953); and *The Curious Death of the Novel* (Baton Rouge: Louisiana State University Press, 1967). One should consult also Rubin's essay "Second Thoughts on the Old Gray Mare: The Continuing Relevance of Southern Literary Issues," in George Core, ed., *Southern Fiction Today: Renascence and Beyond* (Athens: University of Georgia Press, 1969).

Other writings on the relationship of southern letters to regional thought are vital to a study of the Lost Cause. C. Hugh Holman's *Three Modes of Modern Southern Fiction: Ellen Glasgow, William Faulkner, Thomas Wolfe* (Athens: University of Georgia Press, 1966) is provocative. See also Holman's essay "The View from the Regency-Hyatt: Southern Social Issues and the Outer World," in Core, ed., *Southern Fiction Today*; also important are Holman's "The Southerner as American Writer," in Charles G. Sellers, Jr., ed., *The Southerner as American* (Chapel Hill: University of North Carolina Press, 1960), and "A Cycle of Change of Southern Literature," in John McKinney and Edgar Thompson, eds., *The South in Continuity and Change* (Durham, N.C., Duke University Press, 1965).

Critic and novelist Walter Sullivan questions the continuation of the Lost Cause mentality in a long, pleasant debate with Louis Rubin, Jr., in *Death by Melancholy: Essays on Recent Southern Fiction* (Baton Rouge: Louisiana State University Press, 1972) and in a series of stimulating essays, including "The New Faustus: The Southern Renascence and the Joycean Aesthetic," in Core, ed., *Southern Fiction Today*. Also extremely valuable is Lewis P. Simpson, *The Dispossessed Garden: Pastoral and History in Southern Literature* (Athens: University of Georgia Press, 1975).

The changing relationship of southern literature and culture has been described in several works of both general and specific nature. Some broader studies of the history of the South have paid close attention to the development of the region's literature. Especially useful are C. Vann Woodward, *Origins of the New South, 1877–1913* (Baton Rouge: Louisiana State University Press, 1951), and George B. Tindall, *The Emergence of the New South, 1913–1945* (Baton Rouge: Louisiana State University Press, 1967). Francis Simkins' *A History of the South* (New York: Knopf, 1953) also includes valuable material.

A number of specialized works have treated various aspects of the relationship between southern letters and culture. Francis Pendleton Gaines's *The Southern Plantation: A Study in the Development and Accuracy of a Tradition* (New York: Columbia University Press, 1924) remains important. The changing southern imagery of the Civil War is viewed through Robert E. Lee's development as a hero symbol in Thomas Connelly, *The Marble Man: Robert E. Lee and His Image in American Society* (New York: Knopf, 1977). Douglas Freeman's *The South to Posterity* (New York: C. Scribner's Sons, 1939) is a pioneer study in the development of Confederate historiography. Robert Lively's *Fiction Fights the Civil War* (Chapel Hill: University of North Carolina Press, 1957) remains the most complete history of war fiction, although some material is available in Gene Baro, ed., *After Appomattox: The Image of the South in Its Fiction, 1865–1900* (New York: Corinth Books, 1963). Other important specialized studies include Edmund Wilson, *Patriotic Gore: Studies in the Literature of the Civil War* (New York: Oxford University Press, 1962) and Shields McIlwaine, *The Southern Poor White from Lubberland to Tobacco Road* (Norman: University of Oklahoma Press, 1939).

The advancement of the Lost Cause ideology in periodical literature is touched upon in Rayburn Moore's "Southern Writers and Northern Literary Magazines, 1865–1890," Ph.D. dissertation, Duke University, 1956. See also Ray Atchison, "Southern Literary Magazines, 1865–1877," Ph.D. dissertation, Duke University, 1956. See also two articles by Atchison that describe important Lost Cause magazines: "*The Land We Love*: A Southern Post-Bellum Magazine of Agriculture, Literature and Military History," *North Carolina Historical Review*, XXXVII (1960); and "*Our Living and Our Dead*: A Post-Bellum North Carolina Magazine of Literature and History," *North Carolina Historical Review*, XL (1963).

The files of certain magazines prove invaluable to a study of the ideals of the Lost Cause, particularly the mentality of the defeated Confederate generation. Among those most important are *Southern Review*, *Southern Magazine*, *Southern Historical Society Papers*, *Southern Bivouac*, *Our Living and Our Dead*, *The Land We Love*, and *Confederate Veteran*.

General literary histories of the South contain important material on the development of the Lost Cause philosophy. The beginning to any study is the impressive work edited by Louis Rubin, Jr., *A Bibliographical Guide to the Study of Southern Literature* (Baton Rouge: Louisiana State University Press, 1969). Important for consideration are two works by Jay Hubbell, *The South in American Literature* (Durham, N.C.: Duke University Press, 1954) and *Southern Life in Fiction* (Athens: University of Georgia Press, 1960).

Some older works remain useful. These include Edwin Alderman *et al.*, eds., *A Library of Southern Literature* (17 vols.: Atlanta, Ga.: Martin and Hoyt, 1907–23); Montrose Moses, *The Literature of the South* (New York: T. Y. Crowell, 1910); and William P. Trent, ed., *Southern Writers* (New York: Macmillan, 1905).

General writing on modern southern literature has been so prolific that the reader is advised to consult Rubin's *A Bibliographical Guide to the Study of Southern Literature*. Another excellent bibliography is found in Richard Gray's *The Litera-*

ture of Memory: Modern Writers of the American South (London: E. Arnold, 1977). Gray's work is important also as a study of changing trends in twentieth-century southern letters. Both books provide extensive listings of works by and about major southern writers. Other important general studies of modern southern writing include John Bradbury, *The Fugitives: A Critical Account* (Chapel Hill: University of North Carolina Press, 1958); Louise Cowan, *The Fugitive Group: A Literary History* (Baton Rouge: Louisiana State University Press, 1959); John Bradbury, *Renaissance in the South: A Critical History of the Literature, 1920–1960* (Chapel Hill: University of North Carolina Press, 1963); Alexander Karanikas, *Tillers of a Myth: Southern Agrarians as Social and Literary Critics* (Madison: University of Wisconsin Press, 1966); Merrill Maguire, *The Folk of Southern Fiction* (Athens: University of Georgia Press, 1972); John Stewart, *The Burden of Time: The Fugitives and Agrarians* (Princeton, N.J.: Princeton University Press, 1965); and Louise Gossett, *Violence in Recent Southern Fiction* (Durham, N.C.: Duke University Press, 1965).

The last three decades in particular have seen a rising tide of discussion of the uniqueness of the southern identity and the prospects for its demise. C. Vann Woodward's *The Burden of Southern History* (Baton Rouge: Louisiana State University Press, 1966) is a touchstone of such literature. Also important are George Tindall, "The Benighted South: Origins of a Modern Image," *Virginia Quarterly Review*, XL (1964); Frank Vandiver, ed., *The Idea of the South: Pursuit of a Central Theme* (Chicago: University of Chicago Press, 1964); John McKinney and Edgar Thompson, eds., *The South in Continuity and Change;* Charles Sellers, Jr., ed., *The Southerner as American;* and John Shelton Reed, *The Enduring South: Subcultural Persistence in Mass Society* (Lexington, Mass.: Lexington Books, 1972).

Other sources that provide insight include Wilbur Cash, *The Mind of the South* (New York: Knopf, 1941); Alfred Hero, *The*

Southerner and World Affairs (Baton Rouge: Louisiana State University Press, 1965); William Peters, *The Southern Temper* (New York: Harper and Row, 1954); Stetson Kennedy, *Southern Exposure* (New York: Doubleday, 1946); Louis Rubin, Jr., and James Kilpatrick, eds., *The Lasting South: Fourteen Southerners Look at Their Home* (Chicago: University of Chicago Press, 1957); John Egerton, *The Americanization of Dixie: The Southernization of America* (New York: Harper's Magazine Press, 1974); Lewis Killian, *White Southerners* (New York: Random House, 1970); and W. T. Couch, ed., *Culture in the South* (Chapel Hill: University of North Carolina Press, 1934). Important comments on the relationship between religion and the southern mind are found in Couch's book, but more specific works include Samuel Hill, Jr., *Southern Churches in Crisis* (New York: Holt, Rinehart, and Winston, 1966), and Kenneth Bailey, *Southern White Protestantism in the Twentieth Century* (New York: Harper and Row, 1964).

Among the best general studies of the South amid change in the twentieth century are George B. Tindall, *The Emergence of the New South, 1913–1945*, and Charles P. Roland, *The Improbable Era: The South Since World War II* (Lexington: University of Kentucky Press, 1975). See also Dewey Grantham, ed., *The South and the Sectional Image: The Sectional Theme Since Reconstruction* (New York: Harper and Row, 1967).

The image of the South in modern popular media until the present has received limited treatment. The best overall description is Jack Temple Kirby, *Media-Made Dixie: The South in the American Imagination* (Baton Rouge: Louisiana State University Press, 1978). For the southern image in film, see Kirby's work and Edward C. Campbell, *The Celluloid South: Hollywood and the Southern Myth* (Knoxville: University of Tennessee Press, 1981). Other useful writings on the film image of the South include Donald Bogle, *Toms, Coons, Mulattoes, Mammies, and Bucks: An Interpretive History of Blacks*

in *American Films* (New York: Viking Press, 1973); Peter So-
denbergh, "Hollywood and the South," *Mississippi Quarterly,*
XIX (1965–66); Finis Farr, *Margaret Mitchell of Atlanta* (New
York: Morrow, 1965); Peter Biskind, "Vigilantes, Power and Do-
mesticity: Images of the 50's in *Walking Tall,*" *Journal of Popular Film,* III (1974); Robert T. Self, "Invention and Death: The
Commodities of Media in Robert Altman's *Nashville,*" *Journal
of Popular Film,* V (1976).

Serious observations on the importance of country music
have appeared only recently. Among the best are Bill C. Malone, *Country Music U.S.A.: A Fifty-Year History* (Austin: University of Texas Press, 1968); John Grissim, *Country Music:
White Man's Blues* (New York: Paperback Library, 1970);
Charles K. Wolfe, *Tennessee Strings: The Story of Country Music in Tennessee* (Knoxville: University of Tennessee Press,
1977); Bill C. Malone and Judith McCulloh, eds., *Stars of Country Music* (Urbana: University of Illinois Press, 1975); and Frye
Gaillard, *Watermelon Wine: The Spirit of Country Music* (New
York: St. Martin's Press, 1978).

INDEX